Investiphobia

Overcome Your Deepest Investment Fears

By Paul E. Puckett Jr.

ISBN: 0983335303
ISBN-13: 9780983335306

Preface

Do you remember that scene in the movie *Castaway* where Tom Hanks (Chuck Noland) is about to pull off a band-aid, and then suddenly — total chaos? Chuck tries to get his bearings, but to no avail. The next thing you know, Chuck is in a partially-deflated life raft, floating in an ocean of fire.

The time-obsessed FedEx supervisor barely survives the crash, spends the next four years alone on a deserted island, and becomes best friends with volleyball.

And, then, it was my turn to fly over an ocean.

After months of planning, the trip to Italy had arrived. That meant flying over the Atlantic at night, and the prospect was terrifying. The weeks leading up to the trip were sleepless and often spent shaking and sweating.

But the reward, (a two-week vacation in Italy), was very motivating.

When the day arrived, getting on the airplane was difficult and an hour into the flight, I was ready to get off the plane. But, finally opening my eyes it became apparent my experience on this flight was unique. Other people were walking about talking with friends. Their little children were playing in the aisles and there was a bar in the back of the plane. Nobody seemed to have any concerns — they all seemed to be having a good time. It seemed senseless to suffer while everyone else enjoyed themselves. So I headed to the back of the plane and ordered a nice glass of Chianti.

Investing can be a lot like flying over the Atlantic at night. People can be so consumed by their fears that they either avoid investing or lose sleep at night worrying whether they have made a good decision. Investing, like flying, is a lot easier when you have the right planning, preparation and an experienced captain and crew. With your destination and arrival time set, you can expect a successful and relaxing investment journey with a safe landing.

Many things may affect investors, like:

The need to make decisions
Wanting guarantees
The need to keep up with the Joneses
Thinking short-term
Expecting perfection
Confusing products
Constant change
Difficulty finding the right advisor
Responsibilities to children or parents

In this day and age, we are all busy and stressed and the extra stress created by our money-related responsibilities often causes us to feel like we are disappointing our family and friends. This is even worse when the person disappointed is You!

Yes, there are a lot of legitimate things affecting all of us. But this book will help you understand how to handle them.

You may not even realize how they affect your investment decisions but the purpose of this book is to help you discover and eliminate the behaviors holding you back.

Every flight begins with a safety presentation to let you know what to do if something goes wrong. This book provides the guidance you need for the rare and preventable investment emergency. It is also intended to help you think more about your destination than the flight!

This is your Captain speaking . . .

"Please listen carefully to following safety presentation and enjoy your flight!"

Introduction

Everything you read in this book is based on the observation of clients by a professional working directly with investors over the past twenty years. Some of these investors are very sophisticated and knowledgeable about investing. But most, by far, are just regular, hard-working people looking for professional guidance in the management of their funds. All of them preferred to have complex concepts explained in an easily-understood manner — and that's all you'll see in this book. Fortunately, you do not need to be an economist or an investment professional to invest successfully. All of these observations are fully supported by a relatively new area of economic research known as "behavioral economics".

It is important to remember you are a human with both a mind and a heart, and with both thoughts and feelings. Emotions are part of the human experience. The roller-coaster emotions of greed and fear, often associated with investing, are difficult to control but you can rein them in. Everyone experiences these two emotions at some point during their life. Some handle them, or at least appear to handle them, better than others. When powerful emotions are not recognized and considered, they often have a greater and, unfortunate, affect on our ability to make sound decisions. This book focuses on one very powerful human emotion, fear. It provides guidance to prevent fear from affecting your portfolio and, more importantly, your life.

Some of the people who inspired this book faced their fears in a healthy way. They are now successfully living their lives and investing without allowing their emotions to dictate their decisions. Some of them handled their fears on their own or with other advisors. However, the fears associated with investing, or *investiphobia*, can be very difficult to handle alone.

Even if you enjoy the do-it-yourself approach to investing, you need professional guidance to discover the impact fear may have on your investment returns. Armed with the principles in this book, however, you'll learn how to find the right advisor and how to invest without fear.

Finally, this book is not meant to be judgmental in any way. Any one of the fears, left unaddressed, will probably prevent you from making good investment decisions. But this does not mean you are a weak person, or somehow "dumb". So it is important to not tolerate anyone, (including yourself), who judge you for any investment you have made—or have not made—in the past. If you meet with an advisor, broker, or any investment professional, and you feel that he or she is not respecting you in this way, then go somewhere else. There are some in the financial services industry who like to *provoke* fear because they can use it to sell their products. Avoid these products and the people who market using fear whenever possible. If there is no reason to live with fear, there is no reason to include fear in your investment decisions!

If there is no reason to live with fear, there is no reason to include fear in your investment decisions!

When you are ready to make changes to your portfolio, take the same approach people take when they begin to practice yoga. If you have ever seen pictures of an experienced yoga practitioner, you can imagine how it feels to contort the body into those positions! There are many positions, some *basic* positions, many of us are simply physically unable to do. However, yoga instructors emphasize in every session that yoga is not a competition with the other people in the room. Regardless of your natural flexibility or physical condition, they simply instruct you to "start where you are."

Contrary to what you may hear in the media, investing is not a competition either. We can all invest successfully. You simply need to "start where you are."

Whether it is yoga, investing, or anything that is important and new, seek guidance from an experienced teacher. This book identifies specific fears that we have about investments, but it does not recommend a "do-it-yourself" approach. Instead of learning how to manage your own money, spend the time necessary to find a compatible and knowledgeable advisor to help you handle the management of your portfolio. Money is an important part of our life— but money is not, or at least should not be, the entirety our life. Guidance and professional support makes sense from both a financial and a personal point of view.

[The second half of the book is dedicated to providing the tools and knowledge you need to find the right advisor for you.]

If you're experiencing any fears that have led to a debilitating case of *investiphobia*, simply start from where you are.

When you think about it, you really can't begin anywhere else. More importantly, let go of the past, especially when it comes to investment decisions that were based on fear.

There is no greater antidote to investment fears than recognizing them and using well-directed planning and well-informed actions to eliminate any affect they may have on your decisions.

Table of Contents

Chapter One

Decisions, Decisions, Decisions

"I know what I'm gonna do tomorrow, and the next day, and the next year, and the year after that."

George Bailey in *It's a Wonderful Life*

One of the most exciting things about ordinary people is that we often have no clue what we are doing or why we are doing it. We leave the house on a Saturday morning for a quick trip to the hardware store with plans to pick up some WD40 to fix a squeaky hinge. We get back to the house around lunchtime after a stop for coffee, a few garage sales and a side trip to the bookstore—and then realize that we never made it to the hardware store. While this may make life more interesting, it also makes it difficult to get things done. On the other hand, life would be boring if people were always predictable and did the right thing.

But all of us are different and unpredictable, and so life stays exciting. Some people never forget the hardware store or get sidetracked from their "to do" list. They fix the hinge before lunch and have the satisfaction of handling the day responsibly. Others almost never get anything done and decades later still have a squeaky hinge. However, they can still lead deeply satisfying lives, because they focus on what's important to them — and squeaky hinges are just way down on their lists.

And so it was for George Bailey.

In the film, *It's a Wonderful Life*, George takes over his father's business, the Bailey Building and Loan. He manages this bank with a deep concern for his customers that is often missing in today's banking environments. The movie is set in the years following the Great Depression leading into World War II. George has a personal crisis that causes him to question the value of his own life. Luckily, an angel is sent to help him understand the significance of his impact on the world. George eventually learns that had it not been for him, the evil investment manager, Mr. Potter, would have controlled everything in the town. Without George, it would have been filled with drunks and hard-luck stories. George's brother would have died by drowning at the age of 10 and never have become a pilot in the military where he saved many lives during an important mission. His wife would have never met anyone and become a fearful, lonely librarian.

But these bad things didn't happen, because George was there. He wasn't perfect, but he was there.

Wouldn't it be great to have an angel show up and show us what people's lives would be like if we had never existed?

The list of positive things that George helped make happen turns out to be a very long one. Thanks to Clarence the angel, George realizes that he did make a difference. The purpose of the movie, besides telling a good story, is to gain a sense of perspective of our own value. We're not perfect, but we make a difference — perhaps even a little more far-reaching that we realize.

But before Clarence showed up, George got stuck. He felt like he had let people down, especially himself. He wanted a perfect existence, free of fears and disappointments — but he learned to find joy in a wonderful life instead.

Sometimes we may confuse the *'wonderful'* with *'perfect'*. When we do not live up to other people's expectations, we disappoint them. Sometimes we do not live up to our own expectations and have to deal with our own disenchantment. Over time, we might even question our own significance.

The movie also shows the irrationality of putting things off and never getting them done. When George gets married, he and his wife buy a ramshackle mansion and fix it up while producing a brood of children. At the bottom of the stairs, the knob on the rail is loose. Throughout the whole movie, George intends to fix this knob every time he goes up the stairs and it comes loose in his hand. He is constantly annoyed by the knob, but never gets around to fixing it—even though he has to stop, countless times, and go back a few steps to put it back. After his encounter with Clarence, however, George gets home and runs up the stairs and, as always, that knob comes loose. But this time, George laughs and kisses the knob before returning it to the rail post and continuing up the stairs.

The only thing that had changed was his perspective.

We can learn from the knob on George's stairs by accepting the fact that we are human. Like George, we don't always get everything done in a timely manner. None of us is perfect.

Think about your friends and family for a moment. None of them are perfect, but they've all had an impact on you and the people around them. You can probably think of a few examples of things that they do well and things that they do not do well. Some of them seem to always get things done. Others are very comfortable just taking their time. You probably can think of a few that fit either description, and probably a few in the middle. In all fairness, even the most consistent person in your circle of friends and family will occasionally do something that surprises everyone.

Now, take a minute and think about yourself. Take an impartial and non-judgmental look at the past week or two of your life. Are there decisions that you've postponed, others you already regret, and others you're glad you made? Like your friends and family, you are only human. Expecting a perfect decision-making record or consistently rational behavior from yourself is just as unrealistic as expecting it from others. We will all make some really great decisions and do great things. And sometimes we make mistakes.

If we cannot predict our own motives and actions in advance, then how can we be expected to know what others will do? Nothing and no one is ever really predictable. The people in our lives will sometimes do things that they do not normally do. Sometimes we know why they do the things that they do and sometimes it just happens. This is not just true for our friends and family, but also for ourselves. While a very normal part of life, it's still hard to internalize and accept, especially when we focus on ourselves.

There is a broad area of science that involves the study of people and how they think — and how they make decisions based on what they think. Psychology attempts to understand how minds work. Psychology has many different areas of study, one of which focuses on behavior. Behavioral psychologists study human actions and attempt to determine how and why they do the things they do. You've probably heard the question, "Is it nature or nurture"? Are we genetically programmed to act in certain ways (nature) or is it mostly culture and environment that shapes us (nurture)? The movie Trading Places is all about the creative tension between nature and nurture.

Let's do a little mental exercise. When you listen to news, watch it on TV, or read it in a magazine or newspaper, what do you see or hear? Think of a news story that caught your attention recently. What was it about? Was there a human-interest angle, or did the report just cover the facts? Maybe the reporters just ran the story, or simply didn't have time to consider the people involved. A less-than-expected uptick in the unemployment rate was *not* good news for the 30,000-40,000 people who lost the jobs that are buried in that statistic.

Too often, the numbers become the story and the human side of investing and business is lost. Understanding this is crucial to what we're going to be talking about here because it is this inordinate focus on data and numbers that makes investing difficult for many people.

Numbers are always rational—just ask your computer! People, on the other hand, are unpredictable and do things that are illogical. At the risk of belaboring the obvious, we must understand that investing doesn't happen without people—and so the characteristics of human behavior must be among the *first* things considered when investment theories, products, and methods are developed.

Many economists have somehow forgotten this. They may speak of consumer confidence, an emotion-laden phrase — but it's still just a number to many of them. When they created their theories, they assumed that if everyone had access to the same information that the only difference in their decisions would be based on differences in their circumstances. For instance, one investor might be looking for additional revenue while another is hoping to avoid more income (at the end of the year) because of their tax bracket. They might choose different investments, given their goals are different—but traditional economists still assume that these hypothetical, investors will make their decisions rationally.

The reality is that individual investors often do things that are simply not rational, and this is not limited to people managing their own money. It may sometimes be difficult to believe, but investment professionals are people too! They are just as likely to make irrational decisions as their clients.

In *The Secret Language of Money,* authors David Krueger and John David Mann tell the story of an interesting auction. In this auction, $100 bills are offered up for bid. There is nothing unique or special about these bills—they are simply $100 bills. The auction has a few unique rules. Like most auctions, the highest bidder wins, but the second highest bidder still has to pay his or her bid without getting anything. All participants know these rules in advance and the people conducting the auction made sure that everyone understood the rules. Bids had to be made in $5 increments.

As the auction begins, people begin bidding for each of these plain $100 bills. After conducting a significant number of this actual type of auction, the average price paid by the highest bidder is $465 and the second highest bidder paid an average of $460. Keep in mind, the bills are worth exactly $100. Everyone had a great time and the winners were proud of their accomplishments—even though they overpaid an irrational amount.

You may have assumed that the people in this auction were just plain nuts. You may still be right, but economists at the John F. Kennedy School of Government at Harvard conducted the auction. The professors who conducted the auction represent some of the greatest minds in academia. More interesting, and more humorous, is the fact that all of the bidders in this auction were investment professionals representing some of the greatest minds in the investment world. With all of these great minds involved, wouldn't it be logical to expect these people to be rational and not pay more than $100 for a $100 bill?

But, regardless of their brilliance, every one of the bidders had something in common. They were all human! They wanted to win! Over the past fifty years, there has been an exponentially-growing realization that the human factor is an important consideration when it comes to investing. In fact, a new area of economics is developing that blends economics and finance with human psychology. This field is called Behavioral Economics.

Chapter Two

The New Psychology of Investing

Dorothy: *Do you think there could be wild animals in here?*
Tin Man: *Perhaps.*
Scarecrow: *Even ones that, that eat... straw?*
Tin Man: *Some, but mostly lions and tigers and bears.*
Dorothy: *Lions?*
Scarecrow: *And tigers?*
Tin Man: *And bears.*

The Wizard of Oz 1939

The Wizard of Oz, starring Judy Garland as Dorothy, is one of the most famous movies of all time. Beginning in black and white, it surprised audiences by suddenly changing to color when Dorothy, and her entire house, arrives unexpectedly in realm of Oz. She spends most of the movie trying to find her way home. When it comes to helping us understand the fears that inhibit us in the realm of investment management, nothing beats what happens along that yellow brick road.

We're Not in Kansas Anymore

Dorothy meets a few interesting characters as she tries to find her way back home. She's off to see the wizard and befriends a scarecrow, a tin man, and a lion along the way. Dorothy misses Kansas. Her friends are also missing something — namely a brain, a heart, and courage. Each of them hopes that the Wizard can either give them what they want or at least help them find it.

During their long journey down the yellow brick road, the four travelers enter a forest and start wondering if lions, and tigers, and bears live behind the trees. Thinking they might encounter one of these large and dangerous animals, they hold hands and quickly skip through the forest chanting, "Lions, and Tigers, and Bears, Oh my!".

If we think about it, there are plenty of lions, tigers, and bears that clamor for our fearful attention as we walk along our own paths in life.

Whatever you do, (or did), for a living, there's a fairly good probability that you might have to attend a meeting. If the meeting is on an interesting topic, well-organized, or includes food, then maybe you might even look forward to it. But what if your boss told you that there was a mandatory meeting for all employees at two this afternoon, and that most of the time would be spent reviewing data on a bunch of spreadsheets. What would you think? Like Dorothy, you might say, "Oh my!"

There *is* a type of professional who actually does get excited about data, numbers, and math - we call them economists! Their reaction to this kind meeting might be very different than most other professionals. An economist would hear that there is new data reflecting some new trends in business, and he might think, "cool!" How do these people wrap their brains around so much numerical data and make any sense of it? The good news is that you do not need to become an economist to be comfortable investing. All you need to know is a few of the basics that relate to you as an investor.

What is economics? Economics is defined by the *American Heritage Dictionary* as:

ec·o·nom·ics (□ k'ə-n□ m'□ ks, □ 'kə-) n.

1. The social science that deals with the production, distribution, and consumption of goods and services and with the theory and management of economies or economic systems.

So, economists are "number scientists" who analyze the production of goods and services, how they are distributed and then consumed. Economists may examine entire countries or focus on a specific industry. They gather data, analyze it, and often develop theories with the goal of making our lives better.

Let's take a little closer look at economics and a few economic theories that relate specifically to investing.

1776 was a big year for new economic concepts. The United States declared independence and then fought Great Britain to earn it five years later after the Battle of Yorktown. But the United States was not the only thing born in 1776. Adam Smith, noted Scottish philosopher and economist, published his treatise called *The Wealth of Nations*. While we were declaring our freedom, Smith's book defined the basis of the free market. Adam Smith is widely regarded as the father of modern economics and *The Wealth of Nations* is still in print and studied carefully. At the time, economics was not new, but the work of Adam Smith helped it become a separate field of science.

Since Adam Smith there have been a number of economic theories you've probably heard of before. Karl Marx wrote *Das Kapital* in 1867, which launched the birth of Marxism. The neoclassical period which followed Marxism formally divided economics into the study of large and small economies. These two separate areas of economics are referred to as macro and micro economics. The most famous economist of the twentieth century, John Maynard Keynes, developed a new approach which bears his name, Keynesian economics. Keynes believed that private industry would operate more efficiently with direct government investment. There were many economists that disagreed with Keynes approach, and favored much more limited government involvement. After the performance of our economy in the late seventies, these economists, led by the work of Milton Friedman of the "Chicago School" influenced economic policy. However, under President Obama it appears the Keynesian influence may once again be influential. Let's continue to focus on economics and the developments that directly affect investors. The debate between these two economic philosophies continues with many economists on each side of the debate.

As our lifestyle improved, economists also began to study the investment markets. Remember, like the United States, modern economics and the markets themselves are relatively new. Our lifestyles now allow many of us to direct our attention towards our interests and businesses. It was not that long ago in mankind's history when most people primarily focused on finding food, shelter, and clothing! Today, in the United States, we are fortunate that many people are able to invest through their retirement plans and savings.

Harry Markowitz introduced Modern Portfolio Theory in 1952 and later won the Nobel Prize in Economics for discovering the importance of *diversification*. Diversification is the process of investing in more than one investment or asset class at a time. The primary technique used in Modern Portfolio Theory is called Asset Allocation. Many money managers, investment consultants, and investment products use some form of asset allocation. Recently they, and many economists, seem to be under the impression that asset allocation is dead. It isn't dead at all. The current justification for it is simply slightly different than it has been in the past.

Another economist, from the University of Chicago, developed a theory called the Efficient Market Hypothesis (EMH). Eugene Fama determined that when markets are efficient, it is not possible for investors to consistently beat the index. Efficient, in this case, refers to the availability of knowledge. For instance, if everyone has access to the same information about the stocks in the market, the market is efficient. If information were only available to a few people, then the market would be inefficient. The Efficient Market Hypothesis is not just about information. This theory also assumes that all investors, when considered as a group, behave rationally. This is an important concept to keep in mind; the efficient market hypothesis assumes that all investors are rational.

Do you know of any group of people that behave rationally all the time? Why would anyone assume that members of any large group are all rational? First, remember that to be an economist you also must be human. Economists forgot, or at least they did not address, individual *behavior* in their formulas and theories.

There is a logical reason why this might have happened. Have you ever opened your closet and discovered that your clothes are too tight? Happens to many of us each winter and particularly after Thanksgiving! The experience may cause us to diet or to exercise, but in the meantime, we need something to wear which gives us a great excuse to go shopping. What do you generally do with the clothes that didn't fit? You toss them, hopefully to charity or to someone else who needs them—but either way, you get rid of them.

When something doesn't fit for economists, they toss it. Human psychology and behavior just don't fit into mathematical equations. When Adam Smith wrote *The Wealth of Nations*, economics was not its own separate science. Economics was more a part of philosophy and philosophers are usually very focused on how people think and what they believe in. But accounting for thoughts, beliefs, and behavior is difficult to do with math. Adam Smith handled this issue comfortably because he was primarily a philosopher. So rather than focusing on math or data, Smith used his theory of the "invisible hand" to address the sometimes unpredictable behavior of people. So, in many ways, Smith may have not only been the father of modern economics, he may also have been the first behavioral economist! If you base everything on numbers and data and use math to calculate everything, then you have no choice and must throw human behavior out of the calculation — or make an assumption that everyone behaves the same way (which EMH essentially does).

The field of economics has exploded since 1950. Behavioral economics is also growing rapidly. Before we focus on the fears that inhibit our investing behavior, let's talk about a few modern economists and their theories. We'll start with the man who accidentally began the debate that evolved into behavioral economics. Ludwig von Mises was an economist who began his career as an advisor to the Austrian Government during the years leading to the Great Depression. Mises was the founder of the "neo-Austrian School" of economics and was a strong advocate for individual freedom and the ownership of private property. After fleeing the Nazi's, he came to the United States where he wrote his major work, *Human Action*, in 1949. Ironically, Mises may have illustrated the need to combine psychology with economics, even though he drew a harsh and definitive separation of the two in his book. *Human Action* was a contrarian response to the philosophy of behavioral psychologists like B.F. Skinner, Harvard Professor of Psychology, and author of *Walden Two*. Skinner believed that people could be conditioned to do anything. In *Walden Two*, Skinner describes a utopian commune where people live happily together as a result of scientific social planning, conditioning, and a "technology of behavior." It is interesting that the psychologist, Skinner, supported a controlled society while the economist, Mises, believed in the importance of individual freedom and private property.

Gary Becker opened the doors to modern behavioral economics. Dr. Becker is a professor at the University of Chicago and wrote in his autobiography, "For a long time my type of work was either ignored or strongly disliked by most of the leading economists. I was considered way out and perhaps not really an economist." His research often overlapped sociology as he studied crime, discrimination, and even illegal drug use from an economic point of view. Becker was a student of Milton Friedman and later a Professor in the Chicago School. He won a Nobel Prize in 1992 for his work in extending microeconomic theory to include human behavior and interaction.

Amos Tversky and Daniel Kahnemann helped bring psychology back to economics. Tversky and Kahnemann compared their psychological models with economic behavior. They co-wrote an important paper, *Prospect Theory*, which used psychology to explain differences in the behavior of investors with the behavior predicted by traditional economics. Kahnemann later won a Nobel in Economics in 2002 for his "integrated insights from psychological research into economic science, especially concerning human judgment and decision-making under uncertainty".

Modern behavioral economics hopes to gain a better understanding of human behavior when money is involved. It is not limited to investing and covers anything involving people and their money. Behavioral economists study personal finance, investing, and money-related topics from a human perspective. They understand the purely rational world of traditional economics, but they also include the sometimes-irrational behavior of investors.

So, there are a few important things that you should know about behavioral economics. The first is that people sometimes make their decisions using their own unique "rules of thumb" instead of rational analysis. The second is that people may make different decisions based on identical information depending on how that information is presented. And, third, the markets are not efficient. Never were.

All three of these themes are at odds with traditional economics because the old school won't recognize that humans, investors, are not always rational. These themes, or basic beliefs, separate behavioral economics from traditional economics. As behavioral economists continue studying the investor, we will all benefit from their discoveries. And hopefully you will personally benefit from their work as it's reflected in this book.

Numerous papers and books have been published in the past decade that explain the concepts of behavioral economics and provide detailed research into the way that people and money interact. Some of these books and their authors have strongly influenced the ideas in *Investiphobia.* They include *Greed and Fear* by Herb Shefrin, *Nudge* by Richard Thaler and Cass Susstein, *Predictably Irrational* by Dan Ariely, *Irrational Exuberance* by Robert Shiller, and *The Secret Language of Money* by David Krueger and John David Mann. For those who wish to understand behavioral economics, any one of these books would be a good place to start.

There are now mutual funds and investment advisory firms that advertise their use of behavioral economics in the management of their clients' money! Even so, behavioral economics is still a relatively new and growing field. It is now also an established area of psychological and economic study that moves us closer to understanding how our investments 'behave' . . . and how they cause us to behave.

Human behavior is influenced by many different factors. Behavioral economists believe that *greed* has a significant influence over the decisions of investors. Their research also indicates that people may make decisions based on other more emotional influences such as peer pressure, individual background, preferences and biases, their ability to handle risks, their perceptions, exposure to advertising and sales material, and many other factors—including fear.

Our fears, and effectively addressing them, is the primary focus of this book. While *Investiphobia* is supported by the foundational principles of behavioral economics, it is not written from a researcher's or academic's perspective. It's based on the observations and the perspective of an advisor working directly with investors. It focuses only on fears—the fears that affect investors, who may be much like you. *Investiphobia* was written to help investors understand the impact that some of these common fears can have on their investing behavior with the goal of providing clear and understandable solutions so they can invest without fear.

So, what is *investiphobia*?

Chapter Three
What is Investiphobia?

Fear has a way of roaming the mind at will. Depression darkens the mind; anger makes it erupt in uncontrollable turmoil.

Deepak Chopra

In every cry of every man,
in every infant's cry of fear,
In every voice, in every ban
The mind-forged manacles I hear.

William Blake

Money is not your life; it is simply the means to the life that you want.

Investiphobia:, noun, The abnormal, paralyzing, and irrational fear of anything relating to investing, investment professionals, and investment products. This condition is characterized by the inability to make sound decisions regarding investments and often causes poor investment performance.

Fear is powerful. Fear can be contagious. You can experience fear by yourself or it can picked up from others. It can be very strong, and it can fade over time. It can appear, diminish, and reappear, without warning. Fear is normal, and all of us experience it occasionally. Fear can be helpful and it can often be a good thing. Fear can be an inner voice that simply warns us we are not quite ready for something.

As we mature, many of our youthful fears often fade away. We know the oven can burn us, but we learn how to avoid getting too near to the red-hot elements. We learn to cook and rarely think of the oven burner—until we have children of our own.

Many times, fear can overstay its welcome. Fear of flying is fine—if you have no desire to travel. But if it keeps you from getting on a plane, it is *affecting and preventing what you really want to do*. When fear becomes irrational and continuous, then it's considered a full-blown phobia. Phobias are ongoing and a seriously-detrimental effect on the behaviors of those who suffer from them. A phobia can paralyze us when we should move — or cause us to lurch when we should be still. While we may come to think of our phobias as simply a part of who we are, they are, by definition, irrational and damaging.

Many common phobias have been identified — some are very serious, and some seem quite silly. There is *Agoraphobia*, the fear of open spaces; *Ablutophobia*, the fear of washing or bathing, *Alektorophobia*, the fear of chickens; *Batophobia*, the fear of heights; *Catoptrophobia*, the fear of mirrors, *Dromophobia*, the fear of crossing streets, and even *Peladophobia*, which is the fear of bald people.

But what if you have a phobia relating to investing? Many people have very strong fears relating to their money. Many are more than just concerned. Their fears have reached phobic levels. In a capitalist economy, one would think we would be very comfortable and open about money — and our feelings about our investments. Yet many people are not at all comfortable discussing their investments. They have fears that have negatively impact their investment decisions. To prevent these fears from affecting their portfolio, they must be open to recognizing what they are, and then effectively addressing them. When fear is ignored or denied, it can become a phobia that will not only destroy your investment portfolio, it will also affect your life.

The purpose of this book is to identify the many individual fears that may cause *investiphobia*, provide examples of the ways they may manifest in your investment life, give suggestions on the best ways to address each fear, and provide guidance on keeping these fears from keeping you from what you really want to do. Like many serious illnesses, you should not attempt to treat your own investiphobia.

Hands down, hiring the *right* financial professional to help you is the best way to prevent investiphobia from killing your dreams. The longest chapter in the book is dedicated to finding the right advisor, and the appendix includes a questionnaire to help you find the best one for you.

The book identifies eighteen specific fears that can cause *investiphobia*. Some may be more common than others, but the only ones that should matter to you are the ones that affect you.

To treat investiphobia, you must address the root causes. It is critical to know how it developed, because the treatment is directly related to the concerns that led the phobia. Some fears may be addressed with a simple investment choice or allocation. Others may require legal or accounting advice. All of them need a holistic approach that takes into consideration every aspect of your life. Money is not your life; it is simply a means to the life that you want.

Many books have been written about how our thoughts determine our future. Ralph Waldo Emerson said, "We become what we think about all day long." According to Norman Vincent Peale, "Any fact facing us is not as important as our attitude toward it, for that determines our success or failure." Investiphobia is a combination of fearful thoughts and negative expectations. We expect our investments to fail, and when they do, we know that we were right. As you examine your feelings about investing, you should begin by expecting your investments to do well. If you do, your fears will diminish, and you're more likely to do well!

Do you have investiphobia?

At the end of this chapter, there's a quiz you can take. This will show you how some of these fears may have gotten out of hand for you. Then, simply read the fear descriptions to see if any apply to you.

As you read about each fear, keep in mind that it is perfectly normal to experience any of them, at any given time. Whether your fears are driven by the economy, politics, or scams, it would be abnormal to have absolutely no fear about investing! It's the ones that are *chronic* that will hold you back in the long run. In 2008, the market plunged and everything looked really bad. We heard about a major hedge fund manager evidently was actually running a "Ponzi" scheme for over thirty years and took over fifty billion dollars of his clients' money. Many of his investors were very wealthy individuals and families. Some of them were charities and many were investment managers who allowed him to manage their clients' money. Many of them were international banks. He was not alone. Many other advisors and brokers have also been charged with violations involving their mismanagement or outright theft of their clients' money. How can we invest our money when the best and brightest cannot manage theirs?

It actually is not that difficult if you use a process that helps you choose experienced, knowledgeable, and, most importantly, honest advisors to assist you. Do not choose managers based on where they go to church, where they golf, or any other religious or social network. Do not choose them based on where they went to school, or the part of the country where they work. The biggest scams are almost always committed against people who never screen their professional advisors because they, or their friends, already "know" them. Make sure you read the section on choosing your advisor and use the questionnaire in the appendix even if you have known them for years.

You may be reading this book while the economy and markets are still down. If so, things may still feel hopeless. After dropping over 40 percent during most of 2008, the market is actually up almost 20 percent at the time of this writing. Funny, have you seen *that* reported on any major network, weekly magazine, or TV show. Of course, if you have been invested for a while, then the value of your portfolio is still far below the value it had a year ago. You may be very hesitant to get back on the horse, and that is perfectly okay! But make sure that your reasoning is being shaped by one of the paralyzing fears described on the following pages.

A beat-up stock market is not a reason to avoid investing. The old mantra, "Buy low and sell high" is easy to say but hard to do! It is even harder if you have some form of *investiphobia*. Again, the first steps out of this condition is to read or scan the fears to see if you might be suffering from any of the fears described. The cures, and recommendations for finding an advisor, follow the descriptions of the fears. There is also a comprehensive, detailed, and easy–to-understand overview of brokers, investment advisors, trust officers, insurance agents, accountants and attorneys with information on what each does, how they are compensated, who they represent, and how they are regulated.

Take a few minutes to score yourself on the quiz below to get an idea how you might be doing in regard to your own levels of investiphobia . . .

The Investiphobia Quiz

1) Is your entire portfolio currently in money market accounts, certificates of deposits, fixed annuities, individual bonds, or short-term bond funds?
2) Do you look at the value of your portfolio daily or even more frequently?
3) Do you check your bank account each month on the due date to make sure your social security check, or your paycheck, has been deposited?
4) Do you worry about your income falling?
5) Do you feel like prices are rising faster than your income?
6) Have you, or your current broker, made more than 10 trades in the last year?
7) Do you watch, or listen, to investment commentators like Jim Cramer, Neal Cavto, CNBC, Bloomberg, etc., every day?

8) Have you intentionally withheld information about your finances so that not even one trusted professional—your attorney, accountant, or advisor, know everything about your current assets, debts, insurance, and estate plan?
9) If something happened to you, would your family be surprised how much they did not know about your finances?
10) Do you worry how your heirs will handle things, once you are gone?
11) Within the past two years, have you bought any investment that you heard a friend say was great?
12) If a financial professional told you that a particular investment was only available for a limited time, or only to those that qualify, would you be more likely to invest in it?
13) Have you ever completed your research on an investment, or been given everything you need by your financial professional, and found yourself unable to make a decision?
14) Have you ever "known" that you should sell one of your investments, but just couldn't seem to make the final decision?
15) Do you worry about how complicated investment and insurance products have become?
16) After you make any investment or buy insurance, are you often concerned that there may have been a better product or solution?
17) Do you currently have any investment that you intend to buy or sell, but just can't seem to actually do it?
18) Do you worry about someone taking your money?

19) Do you know anyone who lost money because their advisor took them to the cleaners?
20) Do you feel like most financial professionals out to "take" their clients?
21) Have you ever followed an investment recommendation that you heard on the TV or radio and later regretted it?
22) If an advisor recommended a new type of investment, one that you had never seen or heard of, would you be unwilling to consider purchasing it because it is new?

Scoring:

If you only have 1-5 "Yes" responses, then you're a "Three-C Investor" (Calm, Cool, And Collected).

If you have 6-9 "Yes" responses, then it's likely your current advisor isn't doing everything he or she could be doing for you.

If you have more than 11 "Yes" responses, then you have full-blown (but treatable) *Investiphobia*

Chapter Four

The Fear of Losing Your Investment

Regret is more than the pain of loss. It is the pain associated with feeling responsible for the loss.

Hersh Shefrin

Loss is a part of life. Loss can help us appreciate what we have more than we might without the possibility of loss.

We've all experienced significant losses in life. You probably experienced your first big loss as a child. Maybe a relative gave you a wristwatch, or jewelry, and you proudly wore it to elementary school even after your parents warned you to keep it safe at home. Suddenly, you realized it was missing and the reality of the loss hit you. Years later, you can afford to buy many similar items but it is hard to forget losing something you value. Some losses we experience as children are irreplaceable. The death of a dog, or cat, or a loved one, is very traumatic for children and adults. Even though these losses are not related to money, the experience of loss can affect your ability to make sound decisions involving any investment with the potential for loss.

It is not something that any rational person would want to see repeated. But loss is a part of life. Loss management and prevention is also a part of life. The possibility of loss can help us more deeply appreciate what we do have — and what we have not lost.

As investors, we have myriad choices for our hard-earned cash. Most of these options are not guaranteed. You may be terrified of losing some, or even all, of your money. The greater your fear of loss, the more limited your choices will be. If you are absolutely determined to never lose money, then only guaranteed choices, with very low returns on your investment, can be selected.

Of all the fears, the fear of loss is possibly the most common cause of investiphobia — and the most preventable. Of course, the younger you are when you experience a loss, the more likely you are to recover it. If you are currently an income earner, you can make up for investment losses with additional cash flow. But if you are retired, you not only have fewer years, you also probably do not want to be forced by poor investment decisions to work again.

Losses you've experienced — or heard about from family members, friends, or even in the news — are difficult to swallow. They create stress and anxiety as you think of your current investments, and can prevent you from making profitable decisions. You might decide to avoid investing completely by just using banks, credit unions, or even your mattress! Or, you might decide that it's just too risky to make any change to your portfolio and keep your existing investments regardless of their anemic performance. That may not seem logical, but *irrational fears rarely cause rational behavior.*

Fear of loss is the most common cause of *investiphobia*, but it is also easily cured. A skilled and trustworthy advisor will help you determine your comfort-levels when it comes to how much you need to risk.

The fear of loss is possibly the most common cause of investiphobia—and the most preventable.

Chapter Five

The Fear of Losing Income

When it comes to interest rates, investors are particularly slow learners.

Hersh Shefrin

Most people have three basic time periods in their lives during which a source of income provides for their needs. During the first years of life, parents take care of their children. They made sure that we had food to eat, clothes to wear, and a roof over our heads. Parents have a responsibility to provide for their children, and any worries associated with income are usually not of great concern to little people. Kids have plenty of things on their minds, and their worries are usually more oriented towards their friends and school than on their parents' income. Most children don't really know what income is! But their parents are responsible for training them to become self-sufficient and independent. Eventually, they're hearing and answering that famous question, "What do you want to be when you grow up?" They begin to explore their interests, and learn more about jobs and careers (reflecting those interests), preparing them to generate their own incomes.

Eventually, they will leave their childhood home and support themselves in a job or career of their choosing. This is where the second income phase begins. They may be little or great anxiety as they make the transition from dependence on their parents to dependence on themselves. They may marry, have children, and become responsible not only for themselves but also for their own kids. For most of them, the primary source of income is usually a salary or hourly wage. They may be concerned about getting laid off—and so they may keep a reserve to cover expenses in times of unemployment.

They may also start saving money for the third income phase, retirement, in their investment portfolios. If they're lucky, they will be healthy enough to retire and enjoy this third phase of their lives. During this last period, it is their savings, investments, pensions, and social security that will be expected to provide a happy retirement for them, as well as for those who may still depend on them.

Some retirees depend entirely on their social security check to provide the income they need for food, shelter, clothing, and healthcare. If they saved and invested during their working years, they might able to maintain more independence by generating income from their retirement plans and investments. When asked, most seniors can easily and quickly tell you the amount of their Social Security check and the date that it is deposited into their account. They paid into the system for many years to earn it, and many check their bank accounts on the payment date to make sure that the deposit is there. Most retirees in this position often feel like they have less control over their income than they did during their working years. Most would prefer to spend their time enjoying their hobbies and grandchildren, but poor investment decisions or a lack of savings can force them to significantly reduce their standard of living or return to work.

It's ironic, but I've noticed that there's a direct relationship between the size of a person's portfolio and his or her anxiety levels! Most of the people who have money are far more likely to be consumed with worry than those who have only Social Security! This group of affluent retirees has less time to recover from investment losses. Even people with millions of dollars can be wracked with the fear that they may lose their income. In contrast, there are happy people who live with only their monthly Social Security check that is often less than a thousand dollars.

What makes the difference between these two types of people?

When you have a portfolio that provides a portion of your income, some fear may be justified as interest rates have fallen substantially over the past thirty years. If you bought CD's during the 1980s, you remember 10 percent or higher CD rates. If you spent all of your CD income, what happened when CD rates fell to 8 percent, 5 percent, 3 percent, and so on? Going from 10 percent to 3 percent is a 70 percent pay cut!

Fear of losing income is perfectly normal—and manageable. However, some retired investors lose sleep, and their health suffers, because they can't stop dwelling on the potential threats to their income. If you worry about your income on a daily basis, you've got *investiphobia*.

Which, of course, is entirely treatable. An advisor can be a very helpful ally to help you feel comfortable buying and holding investments with the potential for growth of principal. You will need this growth to help maintain your income against the single biggest cause of income loss – inflation.

Chapter Six
The Fear of Inflation

"Inflation is as violent as a mugger, as frightening as an armed robber and as deadly as a hit man."

Ronald Reagan

Our lives and our investments would be so much easier if it were not for inflation. Can you remember when gasoline sold for less than fifty cents per gallon and a cup of coffee was just quarter or less? Today a cup of coffee— not to mention a venti quad shot skinny cinnamon dolce — costs a lot more money than just a few years ago. The problem with inflation is it diminishes our spending power.

For older retirees, inflation is not just a hypothetical term. Some remember gasoline at less than one dollar a gallon and new cars for much less than $20,000. The income they received when they began retirement in the 1980s or 1990s has already been impacted by inflation. Social Security increases with the Consumer Price Index, but there is no such automatic increase for CDs, bonds, stocks, and the like. The dramatic increase in gasoline prices in 2008 caused many a sleepless night for American retirees.

The older you are, the more you have seen prices increase. During our working years, we kept pace with inflation with annual raises and promotions. When we retire, it is our portfolios that need to generate our annual raises. Surprisingly, many people either forget or ignore the impact of inflation on their retirement. But, there are also people who cannot stop thinking about the impact of inflation because the spending power taken away by inflation can be just as traumatic as the actual loss of principal.

Planning for inflation could be easier if we could project it accurately. Predicting the weather is easier than guessing the future inflation rate. We just don't know what will happen in the future. We have to guess based on history and the opinions of economists and other experts.

Even so, it's absolutely necessary to consider inflation in your investment strategies. We know that inflation *can* impact our spending power but we do not know *when* it will occur or *how dramatically* it may affect our income. These are the unknowns that cause some retirees to be overly preoccupied. The symptoms of this type of *investiphobia* are very different from the fears of losing money or income.

When you develop a paralyzing fear about the loss of spending power, you typically have an obsession with inflation. Instead of looking for safety, you crave the growth that can offset the impact of inflation. This can result in a portfolio that is much requires far too much risk. Investors who suffer from this type of investiphobia will often trade regularly and invest too heavily in the stock portion of their portfolio. For them, investing is not the issue. They often hold very little in emergency funds, bank accounts or cd's to remain fully invested in equities — even when they are in their seventies or eighties.

Chapter Seven
The Fear of Thinking Long-Term

When you obsess over how your investment is doing from day-to-day or week-to-week, you could be more tempted to tinker with it instead of sticking to your long-term diversified plan. Not to mention, you'll probably lose sleep.

Erin Burt, Kiplinger.com,
March 13, 2008

***Asset allocation**, not stock-picking, not sector funds, not guessing the direction of the Dow Jones averages, is the key to financial success.* Jim Cramer, Intro to *The Little Book that Saves Your Assets*,

by David Darst

One of the most popular investment shows on TV is the Jim Cramer show, Mad Money. If you have watched the show, you have probably heard the question, "Is your portfolio ready for Monday?" Jim Cramer is a highly-successful investor, writer and TV showman. His question seems to capitalize on the extreme short term and this is not uncommon. We all seem to need answers for time periods that really should not be relevant to our investments. A better question might be:

"Is your portfolio ready for 2018?"

On the Today Show a few years ago, Cramer created a controversy by looking into the camera and saying "Whatever money you may need for the next five years, please take it out of the stock market right now, this week. I do not believe that you should risk those assets in the stock market right now." The reaction by many in the financial services field, and the media, was one of outrage and shock. How could he could be so dramatic, vocal, and short-term in his thinking?!? However, there are very few reputable investment professionals who would disagree with the advice in Cramer's quote. You should not invest in the markets for short-time periods. The stock market provides tremendous growth over the long-term, but in exchange for the growth you must accept short-term risks. If anything, you should be thinking in terms of at least ten to fifteen years when investing in the stock markets.

The portion of your money that you put into stocks should be long-term money. So if you think about it, Jim Cramer was correct: investing short-term money in the stock market is something you should not do. If you have money in the market now that you know you will need within the next ten years, then you should probably talk to your advisor about a safer investment for this portion of your portfolio. He or she will probably recommend high-quality bonds, certificates of deposit, and other guaranteed savings and investments to balance your existing positions in equity mutual funds.

There is too much focus on the short term in our society. When it comes to investing, most people have difficulty thinking long-term because the financial services industry often has a focus on the what's happening this week. Brokers, brokerage firms, and product providers need to sell new products—most of which will be purchased using proceeds from the sale of another investment product. While there are legitimate improvements to products that should be considered as replacements for your current investments, this should only be something you consider on an annual basis when your advisor rebalances your portfolio. There is no reason for a continuous and active turnover of your portfolio, particularly if it is driven by the availability of new products.

There are a lot of people who make a lot of money getting you to think short-term. Most investment products are designed to make you feel safe from losing principal, income, or to reduce your income taxes. Although this can be a good thing, the financial services industry has created a difficult environment by taking it too far. As an example, consider one of the most popular long-term products on the market today: variable annuities. Look at how often this product is revised and how some managers tap into short-term fears to sell this product.

Variable annuities make you feel safe by deferring income taxes as long as you do not withdraw anything from the account. They are convenient as they are available at most brokerage firms and can be held in your regular brokerage account. They may also provide a guaranteed level of withdrawal, even if their value drops to zero. Variable annuities often provide a death benefit to protect your heirs if the annuity is worth less than you paid at the time that you pass away. They also often have an option to provide an income based on either your original purchase price, or a higher value established on the gain in the product on future dates.

In reality though, many of these products are expensive, have lengthy surrender periods, and may not actually protect you from short-term market movements or income taxes. Variable annuities have very high expenses in comparison to most other products. They pay higher-than-average commissions to the brokers who sell them, and they are frequently phased out as new variable annuities are introduced to replace them.

Although they are tax-deferred, if you are in the higher income tax brackets when you withdraw from your variable annuity, you may actually pay more in taxes! All income withdrawals from an annuity are treated for tax purposes as ordinary income. With the current capital gains rate substantially lower than the ordinary income tax rate, you may actually be converting capital gains to ordinary income and effectively doubling your tax! The minimum withdrawal rate helps guarantee your income, but the entire annuity may disappear from your estate and leave your beneficiaries with nothing.

It is also important that your advisor demonstrate the actual withdrawals when you choose the guaranteed life benefit, withdrawal option, or lifetime income rider. All of these terms represent the same benefit, but they may have different names depending on the insurance company who provides the annuity. You usually pay additional expenses for this privilege and you should know what you receive in exchange for paying higher expenses. At this time, these riders usually guarantee a withdrawal rate of 6% of the original investment. Some contracts allow a "step-up" to a higher value if the variable annuity grows before you begin withdrawing and this increases your income. Remember that with any annuity, you must be at least 59 ½ years old when you begin your withdrawals to avoid penalties.

As an example, suppose you purchase a variable annuity for $100,000 and you lock in a step-up in value when it gets to $120,000. Also assume that you begin withdrawals at age

65 and that you use the guaranteed income with a withdrawal rate of 6%. Generally speaking, once you begin withdrawing, you must continue to make withdrawals at this rate until you pass away. Based on $120,000, you would receive $600 per month and it will take 16.67 years to get back your $120,000 investment. If you start these withdrawals at age 65, you will be almost 82 when you begin receiving something other than your starting value! What if you decided to begin withdrawing at age 75? You would be almost 92 before you recovered your investment!

Now, given the extra expenses, does it still sound like a great deal?

There may be an appropriate variable annuity for your circumstances, but this product should be examined very closely before considering purchase. If you work with a broker, consider including your CPA or planner in your decision.

It is also important to remember that the massive amount of data available about all investments and the markets can be mentally straining. Some of us are made to feel a constant need to change our investments, buy something new, or sell our current investments. At the least, we feel pressure to think about our portfolio and investments on a weekly basis, or even more often. The Internet makes it easy to do this. The Web allows us to track our returns at the individual security level and across our portfolio. The big banks and brokerage firms often offer tracking tools that can include our bank accounts, credit cards, mortgages, investments, and even our retirement plans. They can be a very useful tool for tracking your investments and monitoring your broker or advisor. But if you make a decision on where to eat lunch based on the change that your net worth may have experienced in the past twenty-four hours, this otherwise-useful tool may be causing you to focus too much on the short term. The proper use of these services is to keep an eye on your accounts and the actions of your broker or advisor. They also provide a convenient "one-stop" source when you need to know your accounts values — which can be very handy when you need to prepare a financial statement or want to measure your performance.

It is interesting that professionals are trained to invest in growth-oriented investments only when the investor indicates that his or her funds are for a long-term purpose. The industry is fully aware of the danger of investing in stocks for the short term. As a matter of fact, your broker cannot invest in volatile funds or securities unless the proper box is checked on your new account form!

If you were truly investing for the long-term, why would you make changes so often? Many people have difficulty, or fear thinking long-term, simply because we are buried with so much information designed to make us feel the need to do something.

Quite often, we would be better off doing nothing!

Chapter Eight
The Fear of Losing Control

We must be willing to let go of the life we have planned, so as to accept the life that is waiting for us.

Joseph Campbell

The harder you fight to hold on to specific assumptions, the more likely there's gold in letting go of them.

John Seely Brown

Do you remember the first time that you realized that you had control of something? Wasn't it a great feeling? You did what you wanted to do, without permission, because you had control. For most of childhood, kids can't wait to control the car, dinner, schedule, and a host of other things. It is the natural indication of reaching adulthood. You cannot be independent without having control.

Like many things in life, control is neither good nor bad. It can be either, depending on how it is used. Some people like to share control, some prefer to allow others to take control, and some people have difficulty when they are not in control. In reality, you are in control even when you share it or allow others to make decisions.

There are people who fear losing control so much that they are unable to contemplate anyone controlling their assets. They may consult an attorney, accountant, or investment advisor, but they never allow anyone to know everything about their financial assets. They may be very bright, and they are certainly aware that they will not live forever, but they simply cannot handle the fact that they will not always be in control. These people have developed investiphobia, and this can cause several investment problems.

Those who fear losing control rarely seek help or advice from professionals. They would rather have control than guidance. As a result, their investment portfolio may suffer. Managing money is not rocket science, but it does require time, knowledge and confidence. It also requires the ability to trust attorneys, accountants, and advisors.

Another potential investment problem caused by the fear of losing control is created simply because people afflicted with this form of investiphobia typically love secrecy. They would prefer that no one know everything about their portfolio. They may even keep their investments and net worth a secret from their family, their friends, their attorney and other advisors. This would not be an issue if we were immortal and permanently healthy. But at any age, it is possible to lose mental ability or sanity. Unfortunately, it is also possible to pass away, actually it is not just possible, it will happen. It is critical to prepare for the possibility of needing someone to help handle even the simplest decisions about money.

There are situations in which people who feared losing control developed dementia and accidentally disinherited their spouses and children. They either gave everything to their favorite charities or spent beyond their means without realizing what they were doing. As a result, their loved ones suffered unnecessarily because of their fear of losing control.

Trusting others and delegating some of the duties associated with wealth may be difficult but it offers many benefits. During our lifetimes, delegating some of the tasks involved in handling wealth frees people to do things that they enjoy. It also may save taxes! Total disclosure and a CPA are necessities for wealthy investors given the complexity of the tax code.

People who worry they will lose control are usually very bright and capable. For most of their lives, they enjoy the knowledge that they can handle whatever life throws their way. Eventually, the thought of their own mortality or disability may cause concern and worry. Not only will there come a time when we are no longer able to maintain control, there will come a time when we will no longer be here! We can control what we eat, take vitamins, and exercise, but we will all ultimately pass. Mark Twain famously said, "Only two things in life are certain; death and taxes". He was right!

Many of us may experience a loss of physical or mental control in the years leading to our deaths. We may have to depend on family and the medical system for our needs. Many people worry about aging, disability, and death. But it is not only death that most people fear; it is the knowledge that everything we have worked for and all that we have accumulated will one day pass to others. Nothing is permanent.

Many people who accomplished great things over their lifetime have become very comfortable handling almost all aspects of their lives. When they look back, they should be proud of the decisions they made that led to their success. Often it is the most successful people who begin to fear that they will one day lose control and have to allow others to handle things for them. Having conquered so many challenges in their lifetimes, they may find that their biggest challenge is planning for the time when they are no longer able to handle things independently.

If you are experiencing investiphobia as a result of the fear of losing control, you should hire an advisor and an experienced estate planning attorney to help you. Initially, only allow them to make recommendations. As you grow more comfortable, you may consider giving more authority to the advisor. But the primary cure for your fear of losing control is not an investment plan or investment product. The best treatment for the fear of losing control is to plan ahead and pick someone to handle things for you. Basically, you need a substitute.

Teachers sometimes must miss their classes and the principal calls a substitute teacher to fill in for them. Teachers are required to leave plans for unanticipated absences so there is always a lesson plan for these substitutes. The substitute is responsible for carrying out the teacher's lesson plan and the teacher and school administration trust them to handle the class and follow their instructions. These lesson plans let the substitute know what classes they are teaching, and what duties they must handle. Often, these plans were simply handwritten on a legal pad.

This legal pad is actually a very simple form of a trust! The teacher creates the trust by writing the instructions for the substitute teacher who replaces them for the day. The substitute accepts the responsibility and follows the teacher's instructions. The teacher trusts the substitute to follow their instructions. The teacher is still in control, even though they are not in the classroom.

Those who have investiphobia due to the fear of losing control can create a revocable living trust and rest secure in the knowledge that their assets will be handled according to their wishes. "Revocable" means that the creator, or grantor, of the trust can change it at any time as long as they are able. "Living" means that the trust is created during the grantor's lifetime. "Trust" refers to the legal document that names the grantor and the trustee and provides the instructions for the administration and management of the trust.

A revocable living trust allows you to control your assets even when you are disabled and after you die? Many of the trusts managed by banks and trust companies were created long before the bank trust officer was born. Even though decades had passed, the trust document described how the original owner wanted the money distributed to successive generations. Some trusts simply instruct the bank to distribute income quarterly, while other trusts were much more specific and more restrictive about distributions.

Some trusts require a review of the beneficiaries' financial or medical circumstances to determine the amount of any distribution. Recently, drug clauses have become popular in trust documents. A drug clause requires the trustee to verify that the child or grandchild is not using drugs before they are allowed to receive any money from the trust. Isn't it amazing that someone who died a decade ago can still control their money?

A trust is a useful tool for maintaining control; but, to create a trust, you must be willing to confront two very basic fears that many people experience. You must be willing to consider that you may become disabled and need help handling your day-to-day needs. Even though you may never become disabled, you know that you will ultimately die. But many people refuse to even consider an event they know will happen. None of us knows when, or how, but we know it will happen. A trust allows your wishes to continue despite disability or even death!

If you suffer from investiphobia due to the fear of losing control, it can be easier to consider your own death than to recognize that one day someone else will own your things and control them. The creation of a trust can generate a wonderful feeling of freedom. You know the day will come when someone will be following your instructions even though you are gone from this earth! You cannot take it with you, but you can still control things if you are willing to delegate. If you are more concerned about death than losing control, you still may find comfort in knowing that a plan is in place to protect your loved ones. These trusts also are a wonderful tool when you travel. Your trustee can handle all of your bills and take care of your assets while you are gone!

This one simple step, the creation of a trust, has helped many of people gain a sense of control knowing their instructions will be followed even after they are gone. You need a knowledgeable and experienced trusts and estates attorney to help you create a trust. Do not use the attorney who handled your last real estate closing or your company business! Once you are gone, it can be very difficult and expensive for your loved ones to change a poorly drafted trust. If you are going to create a trust, use a specialist. Make sure there are several people equally responsible for handling your trust by naming a family member as co-trustee and having an investment advisor manage the portfolio. It is rare for any individual to intentionally steal from a client, but it is even more unlikely when more than one person is involved.

Remember, you can remain in control even after you create a trust. The trust is simply a legal term for your instructions. Even if you do not suffer from control-related investiphobia, you should consider creating a trust. To find an attorney who specializes in the trust and estate area, visit the website www.naepc.org.

Chapter Nine

The Fear of Not Keeping Up With the Joneses

Do not judge by appearances—a rich heart may lie under a poor coat.

Old Scottish Proverb

"Is Keeping Up With The Joneses' Killing Us?",

Headline in *Business Week*, May 25, 1998

"We are impoverishing ourselves," she writes, "in pursuit of a consumption goal that is inherently unachievable."

Interview with Juliet Schor,
Business Week, May 25, 1998

Never make an investment just to keep up with the Joneses.

The Joneses must be the richest, fastest, strongest, smartest, best human beings on the planet. That would explain why we are constantly reminded by our parents, school teachers, and mentors that it would be wrong, absolutely wrong, to even attempt to keep up with them!

Many people are concerned about outside appearances, for some it is their biggest priority. If their neighbor gets a boat, they need a bigger or faster boat. If their best friend takes a cruise, then they develop a sudden interest in travel. This is true for investors who are terrified they are not keeping up with other people.

The financial services industry knows many people want to feel like they are getting more than everyone else. So, their commercials target those who want to keep up with the Joneses. Picture a slim, well-dressed guy named John on the golf course. He is talking with his chubby, not-so-well-dressed buddy, Steve, about the great tip that he received from his broker. His buddy, Steve, wishes that he was lucky enough to have a broker like John's because then he would be happy, well-dressed, and slim. As the background music gets louder a beautiful woman, shown in slow motion, gives John a hug to congratulate him on his great game. As John gives Steve a sympathetic wink there is a tagline that says something like, "Don't be like Steve; you can be like John simply by calling ABC & Company at 1-800-PERFECT."

Think about the real message behind this ad. What is being advertised? Notice that there is no mention of an investment product or service, just a happy guy whose account is with ABC—and a sad, pathetic character who apparently has no direction in life and certainly no women running toward him in slow motion to congratulate him on his most recent successes. This is the message: You will be happier than your friends, in fact, envied by them, simply by doing business with ABC. If this is compelling to you, then you may very well have a form of investiphobia that keeps pushing you to keep up with the Joneses.

People often ask financial professionals what they think about a particular investment. They often reference a friend or neighbor who was raving about it. More than often, it's not a good choice for their portfolio, but they still want it because their friend owns it. And they want a little bigger stake in the investment than their friend. Like the advertisement described above, it isn't about the product at all. It's purely about status and their perception of how they will feel about themselves once they have it in their portfolio. If you have this compelling need, ask yourself a few questions: When you bought the last investment to keep up with the Joneses, did it make you happy? If so, for how long? Did Mr. or Mrs. Jones even notice what you had done, or even cared nearly as much as you did?

During the course of writing this book, there was a great example of what can happen when "keeping up with the Joneses" determines what you have in your portfolio. Over fifty *billion* dollars was acquired from investors by a certain hedge-fund manager. His clients were well-known people. Many chose him to manage some, or all, of their money because some "friend" recommended him over a round of golf or lunch at one of his country clubs. Many chose him because he was in their religious community. Very few of them had any idea how he was investing the money, or the scams behind his trading.

When the fear you will not keep up with the Joneses is driving your investment decisions, you are at a high risk for an investment scam. My high school swimming coach always said not to worry about the competition in the other lanes. "Looking costs you time!" He knew his swimmers would perform better when they focused on the only thing that they could control: themselves. He didn't want his swimmers to worry about the other competitors. He wanted us to focus on doing our best.

Perhaps your friends invest their money wisely, but you should resist the urge to look in their 'lanes'. Focus on your goals. The Jones may not share the same goals that you have. Following your friends' will lead you to their destination. That destination may not be where you intended to go!

Invest your money in a manner that fits your needs with a professional you trust. Use the questionnaire in this book to find a good advisor, and above all else, make sure you understand what he or she will do with your money. Never make an investment to keep up with somebody else — just let the Joneses do whatever they're going to do . . . and stay in your lane.

Chapter Ten
The Fear of Making Mistakes

If you obsess over whether you are making the right decision, you are basically assuming that the universe will reward you for one thing and punish you for another.

Deepak Chopra

Even the best Wall Street investors make mistakes.

Hersh Shifrin

Mistakes are important because we learn more from them than our successes. For some mistakes, we get immediate feedback that results in that particular mistake never happening again. For others, we may not realize we have even made a mistake until many years later. Most people know they make mistakes, and a lot of them have difficulty admitting it. Some people are so terrified they might make a mistake that they are unable to make decisions—which, in itself, may be the most detrimental of all mistakes!

Investing offers the unique opportunity to make a mistake and to know exactly what it costs! As a result, it is very tempting to avoid decisions or remembering ones that worked. Have you ever completed your research on an investment and found yourself unable to move forward? Sometimes we should just listen to our intuition. But if we regularly find ourselves unable to make decisions about new investment recommendations, we should consider whether the fear of simply making a mistake is holding us back. When you consider a particular investment recommendation, you should talk with your advisor until you understand it thoroughly. Once you have the information you need, just make the decision. If it turns out to be a mistake, learn from it, and move on.

Of course, managing investments includes more than the decisions to buy. It also means selling. When you manage your own money, there are plenty of opportunities to make mistakes. Those who suffer from this particular fear are often unable to make decisions because they feel they will make a dreadful mistake. So they postpone decisions and rarely change anything about their portfolio. Those who have advisors often ignore the advice, or accept it only rarely—if they're consumed with the possibility of making mistakes. Either way, in the modern investment world, constantly postponing or delaying decisions is not a good idea.

Talk with your advisor if you think this chapter may apply to you. Ask him or her to be patient and to explain everything they recommend. Also, ask them to let you know when you appear to be postponing or avoiding a decision when you already have the facts, and enough information to make an informed decision. If a trusted advisor says you may be avoiding a decision for the wrong reasons, do not think of it as pushiness—think of it as progress!

If you cannot work with your current advisor in this way, talk with potential new advisors about this issue. Ask them how they would work with you to help you evaluate mistakes if they are made. Consider delegating some of the management of the money to the advisor. Discretionary accounts are designed for people who have difficulty making quick decisions. If you worry that giving an advisor that kind of authority could itself be a mistake, ask if they offer managed products from recognized names. Ask the advisor to sit with you, on your side of the table, and help you sort through all of your options.

Just don't make "mistake-free" one of your investment goals. You are human, and you will make mistakes. Yes, an advisor willing to work with you is human too and can make mistakes. But two (informed) heads are always better than one.

Chapter Eleven

The Fear of Buying the Wrong Product

The fear of being wrong is the prime inhibitor of the creative process.

-Jean Bryant

No one should be ashamed to admit they are wrong, which is but saying, in other words, that they are wiser today than they were yesterday.

-Alexander Pope

People deal too much with the negative, with what is wrong. Why not try and see positive things, to just touch those things and make them bloom?

-Thich Nhat Hanh

A hundred years ago, the horse was a primary method of transportation. The first radio news program was broadcast in 1920. Ten years later, television became commercially available. Computers did not yet exist, let alone the Internet—and there were very few investment products. Most people were poor, and our economy was based primarily on agriculture. Very few people had the ability to invest. The lucky few could choose from stocks, bonds, gold, precious gemstones, and real estate. All of these investments were simple and unmanaged. You bought gold, literally, not an electronic version or a contract of some kind. For the most part, investment products really didn't exist.

In 1913, the United States Federal income tax was created. It applied to only a tiny percentage of Americans. But over time, it grew tremendously, and now almost 50 percent of Americans pay income tax. All working Americans pay FICA and Social Security taxes. The tax code dramatically increased in complexity so investment products were created to help people grow their portfolios and reduce their taxes. All of these factors caused an explosion of investment products. We have more choices now than at any time in human history.

It doesn't help that many products are very complicated. Originally the most complex products were restricted to the very wealthy. Now, even the most sophisticated investments are increasingly made available to the individual investor. So, we have more products with increasingly levels of complexity.

It is understandable that many people worry about the investment products they buy. Will it be the best one for their needs? Will they pay too much in fees or will it trigger unnecessary taxes? Will their money be "locked up" for a period of years? What if you need the money before the penalties go away? What if they never go away? (Believe it or not, there are products with permanent penalties if withdrawals aren't handled properly!)

When you review products for your portfolio, it's very difficult to know you have purchased the right one for your situation. People who find themselves unable to make any purchase, out of fear they may buy the wrong product, have a form of *investiphobia*. The sheer volume of available products may prevent them from making any choice at all. They allow the companies for whom they work to direct their retirement plan and they never make changes to their investment portfolio. It is one of the little quirks of life that the very people who worry the most about buying the right product almost always end up buying the wrong one. Fortunately, it is not difficult to develop a process that eliminates the fear of buying the wrong product.

The first step is to find a trustworthy and knowledgeable investment advisor. As previously mentioned, the longest and the most valuable section of this book covers the best way to choose an advisor. Your advisor can help you filter through all the products and provide the services that are best suited to your individual needs. Many advisors are extensively trained and have experience in a wide variety of investment products. They should be able to provide understandable explanations of the investments they recommend—and they should also steer you away from investments that are just too complicated for what you need.

A good advisor will be in the ideal position to prevent the wrong products from affecting your portfolio. An advisor should use a process that begins with your needs and goals and works from *there* to determine what is appropriate for you. Discussing these issues and writing a plan to accomplish your goals can provide the foundation you need to be comfortable investing. This plan is called an *investment policy statement*. The investment policy statement is covered in detail later in the book. In brief, it provides a comprehensive written record of your investment goals and the products that are allowed in your portfolio. These documents take time to create, but they are worth it. A well-drafted and regularly-used investment policy statement is helpful to all who suffer from this form of investiphobia.

Chapter Twelve

The Fear of Buying/Selling at the Wrong Time

Fear always distorts our perception and confuses us as to what is going on.

Prather and Jampolsky

Investors are predisposed to holding losers too long and selling winners too early.

Hersh Shifrin

It seems to be part of the human condition to believe in our own predictive abilities - and, just as well, to quickly forget how bad our predictions turned out to be.

Steven D. Levitt and Stephan J. Dubner, *Super Freakonomics*

Information can help you decide whether to buy or sell, but it rarely tells you when you should buy or sell.

After talking with your advisor, reading articles in magazines, and watching the money shows on TV, you finally decide what to buy. Unfortunately, you find yourself completely unable to follow through. You might see in the paper or on television what the market is doing, hear the predictions for the coming week, and get worried that you might be buying when the market is too low. No, that was not a typo. It is easy to buy when prices are rising. The upward trend makes us feel we need to hurry because we might miss a great opportunity. We think we better get it now before it gets even higher. If it goes up before we get a chance to buy it, we may feel we've missed our chance and are buying at the wrong time.

Most investors are nervous about buying when the market is low because the lowest day doesn't look like a good day to buy. Months later, we can look back and see the bottom, but you just cannot do that on the day that it occurred. On the lowest day, it just looks like an investment that is doing nothing but losing money. It is difficult to buy a falling investment and it is almost impossible to buy at the absolute low.

You may also decide to sell an investment, but you just can't seem to pull the trigger. You really want to sell at the all-time high, but worry that if you sell, it will just keep going up. Of course, selling is the opposite of buying and it is easier to buy an investment than to sell one. We form attachments to the intangible names in our portfolio, and the better they have performed, the more we hate to sell them. Many investors remember vividly, and often painfully, the day they "shouldn't have sold" their prized investment. They often know more about the performance after they sold it than they did while they owned it! Unfortunately, they feel they have learned a lesson and have vowed to never sell again.

This can make investment management extremely difficult.

Another major problem with this fear is that it can be easily overlooked until it's too late. After all, it doesn't occupy our minds until the second we think of buying or selling. People with this fear often say things like, "If I buy that stock, it will do nothing but lose money," or, "If I sell, it will probably double the next day and I'll miss out on the gains."

There is a huge amount of information available for people who have this fear. But, information is not the solution. Information can help you decide whether to buy or sell, but it rarely tells you when you should buy or sell. Like many of the fears that cause *investiphobia*, the main problem with worrying about when to buy and sell is that you end up doing nothing.

There are several ways to address investiphobia caused by the fear of buying or selling at the wrong time. Delegating the decision, based on certain criteria, to an advisor is probably the best way, since it removes the need for you to make the decision. You, or the advisor, might also plan a gradual sale and reduce the investment over a period of months or even years.

Imagine a client who fired her advisor because they sold 1000 shares of Cisco stock at 69 the day before earnings were released. With 10,000 shares, Cisco represented over 80 percent of her portfolio. The advisor convinced her to sell 10 percent and keep it in a money-market fund. She was making plans to move into a retirement community, and needed to create $400,000 in cash within the next year. Her other 9000 shares rose to 72 after a good earnings announcement. A few weeks later, with Cisco at 74, she knew she made a mistake allowing any Cisco to be sold at the wrong time and that she closed her account.

Cisco rose to almost 80 before closing the year near 40. If she had kept her account, another 3000 shares would have been sold in the 70-80 price range before it fell to 40. During the first four months of the next year, Cisco fell to 15. (That year was 2001!) Since then, Cisco briefly made it back to 34 before the most recent stock market decline of 2008. If she did not sell any additional shares, her total portfolio fell from over $1,200,000 to just below $500,000 in one year. She probably didn't make it into the retirement community but she may have been forced to wait until her house sold before making the move.

Her story is not unusual and the risk of having so much in one stock is important to remember and to avoid. That one holding may very well continue to grow, but can anyone afford to risk the loss of such a huge portion of their portfolio?

The potential for bad things to happen in investment portfolios is real. That is why it is normal to have any or all of the fears in this book. But being paralyzed by any one of the fears can be the cause of a major investment problem.

No one— not your advisor, your broker, or yourself—will ever consistently buy or sell at exactly the right time. Find a solid advisor, develop a written plan and execute the plan. Do not micromanage the process, and do not judge your advisor on individual trades. You should measure your advisor based on their development and execution of the investment plan. You will feel better, and your investments should also perform better!

Chapter Thirteen
The Fear of Getting Taken

Barring that natural expression of villainy which we all have, the man looked honest enough.

Mark Twain

To believe with certainty we must begin with doubting.

Stanislaw Leszczynski

On July 9, 2008, *The Virginian-Pilot*, a newspaper based in Norfolk, Virginia, ran a cover story in the business section about a group of local investors who lost all of their investment with a woman they had met on an exclusive Caribbean island. She entertained them on her yacht with fine wine and gourmet food and appeared to be a very successful businesswoman. Over time, she was able to get each of them to invest, and she sent them statements periodically that showed them how well they were doing. Everything was great until one of the investors wanted to withdraw their profits to buy an investment property. There really were no profits, and, unfortunately, the original investment was also gone. Within a month, she was arrested and awaiting trial.

A list of her investors revealed some highly-educated and successful people. They did not deserve to lose their investment, but it still happened. She appeared to be trustworthy and she was very likeable. However, she was neither licensed nor registered as an investment professional. Her company was also not a registered investment firm. We will never know whether she planned to invest for them originally or whether she had planned the scam from the beginning. It doesn't really matter what her motivation might have been. The bottom line is that her "investors" lost their entire investment with her.

When you read an article about a scam like this one, it makes you think about your money and where it is held. You hope you don't have a similar problem and might even call your advisor just to make sure they answer the phone! It is alarming to hear about people losing their money. If it has ever happened to you or someone you know, it can be extremely difficult to ever invest your money again.

There are unspoken fears and there are also those that most people find easy to discuss. People are generally more comfortable discussing the fears that are least likely to happen and situations like the one above are relatively rare. Of all the fears that lead to *investiphobia*, the fear of getting taken is possibly the most public and approachable. Fortunately, there are very simple and basic steps that you can take to prevent the outright theft of your investment.

Although not the first to say it, Ronald Reagan is often remembered for his phrase, "Trust, but verify." Warren Buffett said, "Investing should be rational. Never buy anything that you do not understand." When you meet with prospective brokers or advisors, use the questionnaire in this book. Get to know them and make sure you get copies of their regulatory filings. Go to the SEC website, www.sec.gov, to make sure that the paper you receive matches the information that was filed with the SEC. Finally, if you do not understand the recommendations or the investments they plan to make, go somewhere else. You do not have to know exactly how everything works, but you should have a basic understanding of any investment before actually committing your funds to it.

A few years ago, the Madoff "Ponzi" scheme was discovered. It made the above story seem relatively insignificant, since the Madoff scandal involved over fifty billion dollars and investors all over the world. The Madoff story is more complicated, but the steps that are outlined in this book and in this chapter would have prevented many of these wealthy and intelligent investors from losing their money.

If you must invest in alternatives like these, then limit any investment to a maximum of 5 percent of your portfolio. The total investment in alternatives should never be higher than 25 percent of your portfolio, regardless of what the Harvard and Yale endowments might do.

Chapter Fourteen
The Fear of Bad Advice

There is nothing which we receive with so much reluctance as advice.

-Joseph Addison

No enemy is worse than bad advice.

-Sophocles

No advisor is omniscient, unless God gets into the investment advisors business.

One of the most common fears among investors is the fear of getting bad advice. Bad advice is even worse if you have to pay for it, but quite often, it's given for free. No matter how you receive it, bad advice is any guidance you are given that leads you to make decisions that are just wrong for you. Unfortunately, it is a fairly common occurrence and almost always unintentional.

Bad investment advice can come from many sources. You can get it from a friend or colleague, a professional, or the media. It can be directed at you, or something you overhear in line at the coffee shop. It may be good advice for someone, but it may often be very bad advice for you. This is often because the provider of the advice doesn't know your specific situation. A great investment commercial demonstrates this extremely well, even if it is accidental. A broker from a major brokerage firm is talking to a client at a cafe. A fellow at another table strains to eavesdrop as motorcycles and ambulances go by. Just when the broker provides this advice, a waiter drops a tray and no one hears the recommendation. The ad tells you to call so that you can get the advice directly, instead of eavesdropping on one of their paying clients.

There are so many financial columns in newspapers and shows on the radio and television where advice is dispensed. Often, the provider of the advice is a credentialed and knowledgeable expert. But most shows and columns have time and space limitations. They sometimes do not have the time to tell you for whom their advice is intended to help. Very good advice for the wealthy may be very bad advice for the rest of us and very good advice for a thirty year old may be very bad for a retiree. Investors often want to buy something they heard about that sounds really good. However, when their tax bracket and specific needs are considered, it often turns out to be a bad idea for them.

Sometimes, a professional provides bad advice. For the most part, the investment community has very good people and companies who want to do a great job for their clients. But, overall, the investment world has not made things easier to understand. As a matter of fact, investing gets more complicated every year. There are legitimate reasons for this, such as continuous changes in the tax codes and the globalization of the economy. But as an industry, we often seem to make things more complicated than they need to be.

When a professional gives bad advice, it is usually due to a lack of training and experience or to a narrow focus on a specific issue. This is not uncommon, unfortunately, but it is not difficult to prevent the effects of bad advice on your portfolio. Most professionally-provided bad advice is delivered indirectly by a friend who wants to share the great advice that he got from his advisor.

Bad advice happens! But you should take steps to prevent it from affecting you and your portfolio. Some investors worry so much about the advice they receive they find themselves unable to take any direction. These investors have allowed their fear of bad advice to develop into this type of investiphobia. As a result, this particular form of investiphobia is among the most difficult to treat because it is unlikely they will hear or take good advice.

Make sure you understand the advice you are given, and make sure it makes sense for you. Do not be afraid to ask questions, and make sure all of your questions are addressed to your satisfaction. Make sure your advisor is willing to say, "I don't know." No advisor is omniscient, unless God gets into the investment advisors business! It is important your advisor be knowledgeable, but it is equally important for him to be the type of person who can admit he either does not remember or does not know an answer at a given point in time.

To minimize the possibility of bad advice, make sure you involve several parties when it comes to major investment decisions, such as your attorney, accountant, or insurance agent, and advisor. A group of professionals can "police" each other and often catch unintentional mistakes before they happen.

Sure bad advice happens, but it is possible to sidestep it if you're careful.

Chapter Fifteen
The Fear of Change

We often believe that the fears of the past can successfully predict the fears of the future. The results of this type of thinking are that we spend most of our time worrying about both the past and future, creating a vicious circle of fear, which leaves little room for love and joy in the present.

Hugh Prather & Jampolsky,
Love is Letting Go of Fear

It is better to be boldly decisive and risk being wrong than to agonize at length and be right too late.

-Marilyn Moats Kennedy

Sometimes we know our investment strategy or a specific investment needs to be changed. It may be our goals have shifted or our investments are doing poorly. It may be a specific security should be sold, or we need to fire the broker or brokerage firm and it takes time to find a replacement. Once we know we need to make this change, it may legitimately take a little time to make a decision. If you have a history of analyzing your investments and making changes based on the information you gather, then you probably have little fear of change. But if you always accept the status quo, or you cannot even contemplate making a change, you most probably are suffering from this form of investiphobia.

This is common particularly with people who have used a very successful investment approach for many years. It has always worked for them and they see no reason to change anything. But their situation at seventy is very different from the way it was at thirty and the world is also a very different place. Old habits die hard, and it may be harder to make changes when something has worked well for so many years. Some people lose sleep considering even the simplest change.

We may have difficulty making changes because we have an emotional connection to an investment or investment firm.

Or we may simply think any change will make things worse. It really doesn't matter why we fear change; the cure takes time, patience, and trusted professional guidance.

Given the multitude of new products that are becoming available, this fear is becoming even more common. With new products being developed so rapidly, all investors are wise to evaluate any product or method before committing to any particular plan of action. Analyzing and evaluating new approaches and products is perfectly rational. But many people are paralyzed by even the thought of a new product, approach, or advisor.

Some investors do not even consider trying a different approach or product. Most of their investments have long been held with the same fund family or brokerage firm. They have probably had the account since they were children and the broker is probably the same one who handled their parents' investments. Even their credit card is probably issued by the same firm. There can be valid reasons to stay with a firm for a long time, but there are many people who stay even though they are deeply dissatisfied. It's irrational, but they'd rather suffer significant losses than change.

Avoiding change allows these investors one of life's many luxuries. *They do not have to think about anything.* After all, if they never plan to try something new, and certainly would not consider anything different, then why should they bother to think about their investments? By refusing to even consider change, they avoid the need to review their current situation.

This makes it difficult to help investors who have this form of investiphobia because they may react to any investment discussion with denial or avoidance. They may react angrily at any suggestion that a new investment or approach is needed. The root of their fear is often the memory of a previous investment where they had a bad experience. For those who have been burned in the past by change, it is seems natural (to them) to protect themselves by avoiding any change to their portfolio.

Unfortunately, avoiding change may be extremely dangerous. The old investments may have been excellent choices when you were in your twenties and thirties—but now that you are retired, they may be too risky, too growth-oriented, or too big a part of your portfolio. Some of the biggest investment problems are caused by an investor's refusal to consider that the old scenarios that worked for them in the past are now dangerously obsolete.

It is important to understand and be comfortable with your investment portfolio, but it is also important to periodically evaluate new and different products and services to see if they are more appropriate for you. If you are paralyzed by the fear of change to something new or different, your investments are limited and your investment performance may suffer in the long run.

The best solution to this form of investiphobia is to find a good, fee-based investment advisor. You do not need to wonder about the commission motivating the recommendation when the fee is the same whether you decide to buy or not. It is also important to recognize the difference between a "fee-only" and a "fee-based" advisor. Both have the ability to charge fees for their services, but the "fee-based" advisor can choose to make commissions from the sale of products. While this is perfectly acceptable for many investors, only a "fee-only" advisor is advised when fear of change is the root cause of your investiphobia.

You should also pick an advisor who moves slowly and deliberately. Like learning to swim when you fear drowning, you should ease into the process of making changes in your investing portfolio. It is not important how fast you move—just that you are willing to take that first step into the water.

Chapter Sixteen
The Fear of a Diagnosis

The point is, when we are in a position to make a diagnosis, we all become overly confident in our predictive abilities and overly optimistic about the future.

Ori and Ram Brafman, Sway

Denial begins to end when you feel focused, alert, and ready to participate despite your fears.

Deepak Chopra

As my yoga instructor advised, "start from where you are" and do not worry about the past

Some people actually fear any review of their portfolio. This may seem like an odd thing to be afraid of, but for some, having a qualified professional look at their brokerage statement is similar to a physical. Oddly enough, most people are more comfortable talking about their medical history than the condition of their portfolios! People who need a medical test to rule out cancer are often terrified of the test results. Some are so fearful that they refuse to get the test. They may avoid the doctor and deny their symptoms. These types of phobias are not rational. When the fear of a bad diagnosis prevents an investor from getting a financial review, that fear has already become a form of investiphobia.

The last thing these investors want is a diagnosis of their investment portfolio. As a matter of fact, they will do almost anything to avoid it. They'd rather just not know. They don't want a complete review that analyzes their current situation, because the truth may run contradictory to the mythical perceptions with which they've become comfortable. Investors with this fear are easy for professionals to identify. An investor who fears a diagnosis will never share the full details of their portfolio with a professional. They may discuss hypothetical situations they heard about from "a friend," but they will avoid any specific information relating to their actual investments.

As a result, they become very vulnerable to buying the wrong product! The financial services industry thrives on helping these investors buy package deals. It is easier to just sell them what they want. For the commission portion of the industry, it is also much faster way to make money.

People who are phobic about a bad diagnosis fall into two similar categories. One group does not want anyone else to know what they have done. They just want to know what they need to do so they can self-treat their portfolio. Like the patient who chats with a doctor on the golf course, they want to hear the treatment, but they really do not want the doctor to know that they are sick. Obviously, this is dangerous from a medical standpoint, but it is also dangerous for investors when they do it with their money. The advice given by the best professionals is based not only on their knowledge of investing, but on their knowledge and understanding of their clients. A hypothetical diagnosis may not consider all of the relevant facts that affect a specific client's circumstances. General recommendations, or specific ones based on incomplete details, are often worse than no recommendation at all.

The second group of people who are phobic about being diagnosed have a more severe form of investiphobia. Like the first group, they do not want anyone else to know they may have a problem, but, in this case, they do not want to know either! Complete denial is never a good investment idea. To admit fear, and to seek improvement, you have to be willing to review your current situation.

Like many of the causes of investiphobia, the best solution involves a qualified professional who can accurately assess your current situation, and make the appropriate recommendations. It is very important when you fear a diagnosis to make sure you are very comfortable with your advisor. Make sure this person does not "rub you the wrong way." They need to be very careful in how they review and present their findings. If you fear a diagnosis, you must seek professional investment advice, but take your time in selecting the advisor and once you are comfortable, be willing to do a complete review. *No matter what you find, it is not a matter of life or death*. It is also not anything you should feel bad about. As yoga instructors advise, "start from where you are" and do not worry about the past.

Chapter Seventeen
The Fear of Taxes and the IRS

All money nowadays seems to be produced with a natural homing instinct for the Treasury.

-Prince Philip Edinburgh

I'm proud to be paying taxes in the United States. The only thing is — I could be just as proud for half the money.

-Arthur Godfrey

A fool and his money are soon parted. The rest of us wait for tax time.

-Source Unknown

People used to say the number-one fear of most Americans is the fear of public speaking. Recently, there was a news report that the number-one fear of Americans is now the IRS! We live in a country that responded to British taxes with a Tea Party and a revolution. Of course, now we have taxation AND representation. My, how we have changed!

Taxes are necessary, and how we pay taxes is complicated. The tax code is not the subject of this book but you should be aware that a large number of investing mistakes that had their root cause in avoiding or delaying taxes.

With that all out of the way, why do honest law abiding citizens of the United States reach a point where their number-one fear is taxes and the Internal Revenue Service? One reason is the tax code is not simple and hasn't been in many years. This is very easy to see. Simply take the IRS guide for preparing the 1040 Federal Income Tax Form and read through the entire document. As a result, there is an entire branch of financial professionals who make their living helping us to properly prepare and file our annual returns. How simple can it be when many of us are more than willing to pay someone to handle it for us?

How does an investment portfolio make our tax return even more complicated? Investments create a lot of additional questions. What kind of income did we generate? What type of account did we use? How was it titled? Did we have a gain or loss? What was the basis, or original investment, and do we have a record showing this basis? Obviously, we could continue with page after page of questions like these, but in an effort to keep this short, your choice of investments and your transactions with your investments often trigger taxes we had no idea even existed.

Many clients and prospective clients are paralyzed by a fear they are about to cause a problem with their tax return, simply by rebalancing their portfolio. Some simple investment changes do trigger taxes, but investment decisions should not be based solely on the tax code. The complicated tax code combined with complex investments result in far too many investors developing tax-induced investiphobia.

You do not have to be "rich" or a multimillionaire to suffer from tax-induced investiphobia. Consider two investors, the first is in the lowest tax bracket, hates paying taxes, and invest only in tax-exempt investments. The second client chooses to invest only in tax-exempt investments within a tax-deferred account. Neither of these decisions are good investment decisions. Both were caused by an irrational fear of paying taxes. Neither one of these people received any benefit from these tax-exempt investments and both received less money than they would have in taxable investments!

Members of the financial services profession, at all levels, make more income as a result of the tax code. The companies that develop products that address the fear of taxation do very well. So do the salespeople and brokerage firms that market them. Fee-only planners and advisors, recognize that a fear of taxes and the IRS can cause a client to seek professional help. There are a massive number of people in law, accounting, insurance, and investing that make their career based on the fear people have of paying too much in taxes. Given the industries that have been created and are thriving as a result of our tax code, it would be extremely foolish to wait for the end of investment-related taxation. Waiting for changes in the tax code is absolutely not a cure for tax-induced investiphobia.

This type of investiphobia is not difficult to cure. But if your tax return is the least bit complicated, you definitely need a team approach. Your accountant, attorney, and investment advisor can be your best allies in recovering from the fear of taxation. Ask them to provide you with the tax implications of any recommendations that are made. Also ask them to plan your net income, or growth, based on existing tax rules. If an annuity or other tax-deferred investment recommendation is made, ask the attorney and the accountant if you need to defer taxes. Some of this decision is subjective, in that the future levels of taxation are simply not known. Make your decisions based on current regulations. Predicting market returns is similar to fortune telling, but it is much easier than predicting the actions of Congress, the courts, and the President!

Chapter Eighteen

The Fear of Losing Access to Money

I never attempt to make money on the stock market. I buy on the assumption that they could close the market the next day and not reopen it for five years.

-Warren Buffett

Everyone has limits. You just have to learn what your own limits are and deal with them accordingly.

Nolan Ryan

It is not a matter of knowing the answers; it is a matter of knowing the right questions.

Every day, senior citizens across the United States buy investment products that have lengthy surrender periods. You have probably heard on the news, or read in the paper, about someone who cannot get access to their money because of the product that they purchased. This happens fairly regularly, and it is scary to anyone who is retired.

There was an article in a professional journal recently about a woman in her seventies who bought a product with a limitation on access that lasted for over twenty years. She would not have full access until the age of 105! Someone convinced her to put most of her money into this product. Thankfully, the company canceled her purchase and returned her money with interest. But how was she ever sold on the idea in the first place?

The article did not cover the specific product that she bought. It may be an appropriate product for someone, somewhere, but it clearly did not fit her needs. Generally, the cause of this type of sale is either based on greed or gross inexperience on the part of the salespeople. They probably attended a seminar and heard great things about the product and the commission they would earn if they sold it. They may have even thought she might benefit from it. These products often feature tax-deferral and some principal or income guarantees.

Some of the products that have these lengthy surrender charges are good products, and some are not. Many of us own products with penalties if they are withdrawn "early": Certificates of deposit, IRA's, and 401k's are good examples. In any case, we know there are products that limit our access to our own money. Some people are fearful this may overly restrict them in some way. Some people are paralyzed by these fears, and this prevents them from using many types of investments. They become singularly focused on access to their money and suspicious of anyone who suggests leaving their money alone for a period of time. They are right to be concerned, but they are also hurting themselves more than anyone else if this fear prevents them from investing.

Again, the advisor you select is critical to your success. If you select one who is knowledgeable and compatible with you, you can expect him to be willing to help you understand what you need to know before you invest in any product. But not all financial services professionals are *advisors*, as a matter of fact, most are not. Many are just salespeople, hiding behind titles such as financial advisor, investment consultant, vice president–investments, and other equally innocuous, but misleading and legitimate-sounding names. Sometimes salespeople also have the Certified Financial Planner, CFP, which is a very legitimate designation, but always remember that a salesperson with a CFP is first and foremost a salesman!

It is not a matter of knowing the answers—it is a matter of knowing the right questions. There is a questionnaire in the appendix that will help you in this process. This questionnaire does not require any investment knowledge. In regard to access to your money, you should know exactly how much freedom you have to obtain your money. There should always be enough accessible to handle any anticipated needs or unanticipated emergencies. Whenever you are asked to purchase a new investment, use these questions to make sure you understand what the product will do for you.

Chapter Nineteen

The Fear of Disappointing Parents

Many of us wish our parents could have been different when we were growing up—and we may still be trying to change them.

Gerald Jampolsky

If you equate an investment with a parent, how will you feel about that parent when the investment loses value?

There once was a woman who, every Easter, liked to cook her family a fresh ham. She would always cut each end of the ham off before putting it in the oven. From their first Easter together, her husband would ask her why she always cut off the ends of the ham. She really did not know why and just said that her mother had done it that way. So he asked her mother and she said her mother had done it that way. Finally, after a few years, he got the opportunity to ask her grandmother when they were visiting her at a nice retirement home. He was excited to finally solve the mystery of the shortened ham and asked her why she cut off the ends of the ham when she baked it. She thought about it for a minute and said, "I had a very small oven and never could find a ham small enough to fit!"

Continuing a tradition is one way to show respect for those who came before us—but in this story, two generations did not even know why they were doing it. We often do things without knowing why. Instead of food, what if it is an investment? What if it turns out that a large portion of someone's portfolio that is affected by that decision?

Many people inherit investments from their parents. For some, these investments take on an emotional value, and over time, these investments may actually come to represent a connection with their parents. This connection with the specific stock their parents left them actually becomes a symbol of their parent's love for them.

This issue is easy to find. There is usually a large individual stock that does not make sense in the context of their goals and objectives. Often they will refer to this portion of their portfolio by saying, "Oh, that's Daddy's." Typically, their father passed away many years ago. Yet, after all these years, these investments are still in their accounts! But they are not considered investments by the children who inherit them. In essence, the stock represents their relationship with their father—and out of their love for him, they will never, ever sell it. Sometimes the stock will do well for them, but quite often these emotionally-charged investments eventually fall in value

The original owner would not want their child to suffer for holding an inherited investment for too long. Most parents would want their child to benefit from their inheritance, and to invest it wisely to help not only themselves, but also future generations. When it is a family farm, a painting, or something else that is tangible, it is easy to understand the sentimental attachment. But a line on a brokerage statement is a bit of a stretch, even though it happens too many times to deny that does have an extremely powerful effect on some adult children.

Sometimes it is difficult to sell an investment that has done well. It is much harder to sell an investment that you equate with a parent. For some, selling an inherited investment would feel like betrayal. The impact on a portfolio of an untouchable investment varies widely. The investment may do well in the time following a parent's passing, but years later; it can become a major obstacle to continued growth. It can be an even bigger problem when "Daddy's" investment is losing money. If you equate an investment with a parent, how will you feel about that parent when the investment loses value?

Obviously, it's impossible to talk with your mom or dad after their passing. But if you could chat with them, they might be surprised at the obligation that you feel to hold their stock forever.

Talk with your children about the thoughts you have about any inheritance that you plan to leave them—hopefully many years from now! Unless you really feel they should keep a particular investment, let them know you do not want them to feel any obligation to hold the investments you leave to them. Tell them to keep it, if it fits with their current goals, but to sell it without hesitation if it does not fit with their goals.

It takes time, but it's important to manage your money based on your goals. If you inherited investments remember not to let sentimental attachments force you to hold investments that no longer fit with your objectives. Maintain your love for the person who thought enough of you to leave you something. Ask the brokerage firm to issue one share in certificate form and frame it as a reminder of your loved one. But take the remainder and put it to work for you and your heirs. Find an experienced investment advisor, and let that person help you change the investment to better match your short-term and long-term goals.

Chapter Twenty

The Fear of Disappointing Children

Parents are often so busy with the physical rearing of children that they miss the glory of parenthood, just as the grandeur of the trees is lost when raking leaves.

Marcelene Cox

I don't know any parents that look into the eyes of a newborn baby and say, "How can we screw this kid up?"

Russell Bishop

Keep everything in balance and do not hesitate to take care of yourself. Your kids will appreciate the example you set for them.

In regard to kids, it is the rare parent who wants to disappoint their children. At some point, we all do, but we try to avoid it when we can. Children have a huge impact on our portfolio. From the time they are born, we save for their first car, college, and their first down payment. Many parents look far down the road and make adjustments in their investment accounts while their little girl or boy is still in diapers.

This is all good! You should look out for those little beings that you brought into the world. When necessary, you should make whatever sacrifice is needed for their security and happiness. But sometimes our dedication to those little bundles of joy can have a negative impact on our investments. In our zeal to invest well for our children, we may lose ourselves. Our feelings about what we will leave behind may make us take too many risks or make us cling to safety because we don't want to lose our children's money. You should consider your children's needs, particularly when they are living in your house and still attending school. But, when they are adults, we should remember our own needs and remember that it is, after all, our money.

While involving your children's needs in your investment decisions can be a good thing, you should also look out for your own needs. When you get on a commercial jet, they talk about what to do if the air mask drops from the ceiling. They always say that if you are traveling with young children, you should put your mask on first. Then put on the child's mask. The same advice applies to investing. Take care of your own needs first, and then take care of the kids.

Many people have trouble with this concept. If the fear of losing money is strong when we are considering only our needs, these feelings are even stronger when we think of our children's needs. This can cause us to look for the safest investments. It is often ten, twenty, thirty, forty or more years before we pass our estates to the kids. With a time period this long, you should be willing to take risks in order to grow your portfolio. One day, sooner than you think, you will need the income for your retirement, long-term care, or that European vacation you've been dreaming about.

You should balance your needs for growth with the income needs you will have in retirement. Some senior citizens invest money for their children in very safe, guaranteed accounts like bank certificates of deposit or savings bonds. Others may take more risk in their portfolio for their children and ignore their own income needs because their focus is on the estate they leave behind. Keep everything in balance and do not hesitate to take care of yourself. Your kids will appreciate the example you set for them.

It is very important in almost all investment accounts to invest in a diversified manner. This is especially true in a child's account.

Chapter Twenty-one

The Fear of Choosing the Wrong Advisor

Whatever you do, you need courage. Whatever course you decide upon, there is always someone to tell you that you are wrong. There are always difficulties arising that tempt you to believe your critics are right. To map out a course of action and follow it to an end requires some of the same courage that a soldier needs. Peace has its victories, but it takes brave men and women to win them.

Ralph Waldo Emerson

What I focus on in life is what I get. And if I concentrate on how bad I am or how wrong I am or how inadequate I am, if I concentrate on what I can't do and how there's not enough time in which to do it, isn't that what I get every time? And when I think about how powerful I am, and when I think about what I have left to contribute, and when I think about the difference I can make on this planet, then that's what I get. You see, I recognize that it's not what happens to you; it's what you do about it.

W. Mitchell

Never forget that the advisor is an employee. You are the boss.

The wrong advisor for you is usually very good at what he does. He has a great reputation, solid training and experience, and excellent certifications. His clients receive great service, solid investment management, and pay a fair or below average fee. People rave about this advisor and refer business to him regularly.

But, this advisor can still be the wrong professional for you.

Maybe it would be easier to define the wrong advisor by starting with the characteristics that do NOT define him. First, the wrong advisor is not an advisor who has been covered in the book so far. He's not a criminal who wants to embezzle, defraud, or otherwise transfer your money to his pocket. In general, he does not give bad advice. He does not sell or recommend the wrong product and he does not overcharge for his services. He is not incompetent. The wrong advisor simply does not fit with you and your plans. Basically, the wrong advisor is right for someone—just not you!

Here are a few examples of extremely competent advisors who are wrong for you. The wrong advisor for you specializes in helping clients who are not like you. If you are retired and your portfolio is needed to generate income, the wrong advisor specializes in growth and works primarily with people in their twenties and thirties. Or you are in the highest tax bracket and the wrong advisor works primarily with those in the lower brackets. Maybe you need investment advice and the wrong advisor is the best insurance agent in town. You should work with an advisor who specializes in working with people who are similar to you. That's the right advisor for you!

Avoiding the wrong advisor is not difficult, but many people fall into this trap by worrying about offending the professional with whom they've made contact. It usually begins with the initial selection of the advisor. Even if you are referred by a close friend to meet with their advisor and he passes your initial screening, you are not obligated to hire them. Even if he is a CFP (Certified Financial Planner) and has been working with clients for over twenty years. Even if your friend is very happy with the service he provides and highly recommends him. Even if you get the impression your friend will be disappointed if you don't hire him. Even though he is extremely experienced and passes all of your tests, you are not obligated to hire him.

Maybe you find a few of his speech patterns, his office decorations, what he wears, or the picture of him with a politician completely offensive. Maybe it isn't anything you can identify—you simply don't like him. You may not find the "perfect" advisor, but you shouldn't work with someone with whom you really don't enjoy spending time.

It may feel awkward declining his services and you may worry about offending an otherwise qualified advisor. On the flip side, many advisors, including myself, prefer to work with clients whom we like and look forward to seeing. Chances are that if the advisor sensed during the appointment that the two of you did not "click" he is probably already anticipating that you will look elsewhere. With no offense intended, he may be hoping that you will move on, and it is even possible that he will tell you to look elsewhere.

If he is like most advisors, he also may know of someone who really would work well with you. It may sound odd, but an honest discussion with him might result in his referral to an advisor who is more appropriate for you. Remember that most competent advisors know and often network with their "competition." Again, the "wrong advisor" is very competent— he is just are not appropriate for you. You should anticipate a professional response to your decision not to hire him. If that discussion results in any sort of awkward pressure, then you just received confirmation you really should not work with him. Move on without hesitation.

Remember, you are hoping to hire an experienced professional to handle your assets. Even though an advisor may know more than you do about finances, never forget that the advisor is an employee. He works for you. You are the boss! Only hire an advisor you would want working with you if you worked together at a company you owned.

You may still feel pressure to hire this hypothetical advisor because your friend referred you. If you decide you don't want to hire him, do not allow this extra pressure force you to hire the wrong person. Don't put yourself in a situation where you may be working with someone for many years in a situation that really doesn't fit. In the end, you may even resent your friend for "sticking" you with him in the first place! Please, do what is right for you. It is not easy to disappoint friends, but in the long term it may be necessary. The sooner you address your decision with your friend, the better he or she can accept it. You might say something complimentary about the recommendation, like, "I can see why you like him and understand why you referred me to him, but I don't think he is a good fit for me. He really likes working with you, and I really appreciate your thoughtfulness in referring me. Thank you for thinking of me."

After you hire an advisor, you should expect understandable explanations of her recommendations and actions. She should expect that you will not always accept or follow them. Carefully watch her response when you don't. Every client is different. It is not the end of the world for you, or for the advisor, when you decide not to take a recommended action. When a client refuses a truly important recommendation, the advisor should take a step back to explain why it is critical and the reasons why you might wish to reconsider. If it is truly critical, they should ask you to sign a letter or form documenting your decision. When an advisor asks you to document your decision, it is a subtle, but powerful, indication they are concerned. If this happens frequently, you should move on to an advisor who is more compatible with your needs. If it happens with more than one advisor, you should stop and think about the possibility of the issue being something you need to address with the person who is the hardest to talk to—you! When several people are sending the same message, you should think about the reasons you are not able to do whatever is being recommended. Quite possibly, the real problem is rooted in the one of the fears we've already addressed.

Author's Introduction to Part II

There is often a vast gulf between how people say they behave and how they actually behave.

Steven D. Levitt and
Stephan J. Dubner, Super Freakonomics

Never hire anyone who is going to report directly to you who you do not intuitively just plain like from first impressions. If your instincts tell you you're going to have a hard time working with someone, pass.

Fred Charette

Before beginning Part II, let's review the information covered in Part I. Investiphobia is the abnormal, paralyzing, and irrational fear of anything relating to investing, investment professionals, and investment products. There are eighteen fears that may cause investiphobia and, by now, you may have a good idea whether any of these fears apply to you. If you have investiphobia, the cure is contained in Part II. Even if you do not have any of the fears, Part II contains guidance applicable to all investors.

Writing a book is a very interesting process. If you want to know what you truly believe, simply write a book. The act of putting words on the page may result in a few surprises. That was my experience and it is relevant to you as an investor.

In planning the book, it was my intention to provide guidance to two distinct audiences, with one composed of "Do-It-Yourself" investors and the other with those who prefer to work with a financial professional. Instead of this introduction to Part II, I planned to provide simple and specific investment management advice for those who prefer the "do-it-yourself" approach. The experience I had writing this introduction is important. It provides my opinion about whether you should "do-it-yourself" or hire an advisor.

When I had written almost all of *investiphobia*, I developed writer's block. I had written all of the chapters on the different types of investiphobia that can destroy an investor's portfolio and skipped this chapter and wrote the sections on the industry and the professionals who you are likely to encounter as an investor. I began writing this chapter with the intention of showing exactly how these afflicted investors could invest their funds in a more appropriate and profitable way. As I covered each type of investment and how to use it in a portfolio, I began having difficulty and eventually did not write for over two months.

Unrelated to this, I attended a two-day training session with George Kinder of the Kinder Institute of Life Planning at the Financial Planning Association conference in Boston. George is the father of life planning and trains financial planners around the world in techniques that allow us, as professionals, to fully understand our clients, their lives, and their goals. He began to develop the life-planning concept over fifteen years ago and is dedicated to assisting advisors and planners in more effectively serving their clients. I recommend his book and his training to any financial professional. The book, *The Seven Stages of Money Maturity*, is excellent and is also accessible to non-professionals.

For most of the first day, he talked about the importance of integrity. In the economic environment for the past twenty years, you do not have to search far to find examples in which the simple, but often forgotten, habit of integrity would have prevented financial problems. He defined integrity as the habit of "acting from a place of wholeness and clarity in regard to one's values" and as "a natural state of ethical balance." As he said is, I suddenly realized I was having difficulty writing about investors managing their own money because I did not believe they should manage their own money. I have always felt investors are better served when they utilize a professional, but I did not realize, until then, that I had very strong feelings about investors attempting to manage their own money. As a result, writing a "how-to" book or even a chapter would be a violation of my personal and professional integrity.

I began my career as an insurance agent with Mass Mutual. Prior to taking that position, I really knew very little about personal finance. Mass Mutual provided basic training that became a foundation for me. After a few years with Mass Mutual, I took a position as a management trainee with Sovran Bank, a predecessor of Bank of America. After an extensive training program, I became a private banker and dealt with numerous clients on all aspects of their financial situation. I was given an opportunity to move to the trust department where I learned to manage money, administer trusts, and settle estates. Eventually, I decided to become an investment advisor and formed my own registered investment advisory firm. Since 1988, I have met with many people and discussed their financial plans with them. Needless to say, I have had ample time to observe a wide variety of people and to draw some specific conclusions about the wisdom of managing your own portfolio.

I have seen investors who handle their money well without a broker or an advisor's guidance. I have encountered very few whose spouse was comfortable handling money without professional assistance. I have seen husbands who would never want to handle the money if something happened to their wife and vice versa. So, even when someone is comfortable and accomplished at managing their own portfolio, ultimately, unless they outlive their spouse, it is likely a professional will be needed.

I also observed an emotional difference in people who chose professional management. The happiest people all had a professional advisor in the form of a bank trust department, a financial planner, or an investment advisor. They were able to delegate the very important tasks of money management and financial planning to a capable, well-trained professional. This delegation of the mundane daily responsibilities of handling their money allowed them to focus on the things that they found rewarding. Volunteering in a local school, working with a charity or spending time with their family, in their garden are all enjoyable luxuries they found far more emotionally satisfying than managing their own investments. Almost all of them were more content than any "do-it-yourself-er" I have ever had the pleasure of meeting.

My biggest surprise was wealth did not necessarily indicate financial knowledge. Having grown up in a modest home and in a middle-income family, I assumed that wealthy people understood money better than everyone else. Wealth is not in my background, at least from a monetary perspective!

My grandfather was a very dedicated and happy elementary school janitor who raised three daughters and had a very happy life. I always assumed people with money were also gifted with the knowledge and emotional balance to handle it with ease.

As a financial professional, I discovered my observations did not match my assumptions. Many wealthy people are not only lacking in extensive financial knowledge, they do not understand the industry. No offense intended, I have also seen financial professionals who do not understand the industry either! And there are some who understand it so well they manipulate it to take advantage of their trusting clients. The Madoff scandal illustrates this point all too well.

I regularly encounter prospective clients who have no idea their financial advisor is actually a broker/registered representative whose entire compensation is from commissions generated by sales. They believe a broker is legally obligated to serve and represent them. In reality, a registered representative is required to represent a broker dealer, such as Morgan Stanley or Edward Jones. Their loyalty and legal obligation is to their broker dealer, to the shareholders (owners) of the broker dealer, and to the regulatory authorities to abide by the rules governing brokers. This is very important to understand. Congress may make things better, or worse, as this issue is becoming a topic on Capitol Hill. In the next chapter, I will cover the different types of financial professionals in great detail because this is a critical component in choosing the right advisor.

Sometimes when you attempt to handle your own affairs, basic and important issues remain unaddressed. Many of the people I encounter, including wealthy people, have not developed a well-designed long-term financial and estate plan. Perhaps most surprising, many do not have a will. Others have never reviewed their estate plan and have wills that were written when Reagan was President! Many of them also have only minimal knowledge of investment management. Those who do have more extensive knowledge often say during a review of their accounts things like, "I thought I sold that," or "I meant to buy a particular investment but I must have forgotten." As I meet with people now, and given the many I have met with over the years, it seems most people simply do not have the time necessary to focus on developing and executing their financial or estate plans without help. It is not a matter of intelligence, as many of my clients are smarter than I am! It is a matter of focus, priorities, and time.

It is difficult to live your life to the fullest while handling all of the details. Many people outsource their lawn care or landscaping or hire a maid service to keep the house clean. They may know how to mow the lawn or vacuum the floor, but they recognize that the time they save by delegating these tasks is worth the costs. Your investments are more important than your lawn and your legacy more important than clean counters! It is worth the effort and the financial costs to have a professional partner to assist you. Pay an advisor to focus on your finances and gain additional time to focus on the things that are important to you. In the long run, you will find the help of a professional both wise and profitable.

During the initial writing of this book, the market dropped over 40 percent. Many individual investors either left the market entirely or are simply not opening their statements because they are terrified of what they might find. If they left the market, they will not know when to reinvest, and if they have a time horizon longer than ten years then they should never have sold. During the next year, as I began editing and adding chapters on behavioral economics for this edition, the market surged to gains ranging from 24-75%! How many individual investors were "back" in the market? A survey was just completed showing only 3 out of 10 investor's accounts grew during a time period when the domestic and international market grew between 40-64%!

Investors who work with advisors have a partner to assist them in remaining focused on their long-term goals. The best advisors and planners do more than manage money. They provide professional guidance and emotional support that is very important when the market appears to be collapsing. Your advisor's greatest value may simply be keeping you invested when the markets are falling!

When you work with a great advisor, you can live your life and do the things that are important to you without allowing the market to overly affect your life. In my opinion, even if your self-managed investment return were identical to the return received from a professional, the ability to be free from the daily responsibility of money management would be more than worth the cost.

It is my recommendation that you are most likely to be successful if you have the right advisor handling the details. He should explain his approach and method in an understandable way and you should not hire him until you are comfortable with their approach. For those who are just beginning or who cannot find a suitable advisor, there are several tools available to help you grow your portfolio to the level where it may become easier to find appropriate advisors.

Whether you have a small portfolio or are tremendously wealthy, you deserve and should expect professional and knowledgeable advice. If you choose to hire an advisor, the amount you have to invest will be a factor but there are professionals available regardless of your portfolio size.

Before moving to Part II, a few brief observations regarding investment philosophy and approach are necessary. I believe advisors who use a strategic, long-term, approach are best suited for investiphobic investors. *Strategic* simply means a method that does not change as a result of market movement. I also believe that combining low-cost index funds with actively-managed funds provides a very valid approach. If you are just beginning to invest, begin with index funds. For many investors, particularly those who choose to "do-it-yourself," this may be the best approach regardless of the size of the portfolio. You probably should avoid individual stocks, limited partnerships, private REITs, tactical market timing, and all alternative investments. Simplicity provides comfort, in my humble opinion. If you hire professionals to handle your account, some of these may be worthy of your investment. But, money should not complicate your life. Remember to keep investing simple and straight-forward.

Your investment choices are important, but they are not the focus of this book. The focus is on your life and how you feel about your money. The key to overcoming your deepest investment fear is not found in a product or service. It is within your control, but I do believe an advisor is important if you have any form of *investiphobia.*

If you really want to address the concepts in this book, and you really want to cure your investiphobia, please focus on the next three chapters and learn the best way to select an advisor. Then take the steps to find and form a relationship with a professional who can work well with you. There are many good financial services professionals available all around the world. Once you have found the right one, you can release the stress and responsibility of your money and enjoy your life.

It is possible to manage your own money, and you may have little choice if you cannot find an advisor that you are comfortable with and can trust. If you must do it yourself, consider the Recommended Reading and Recommended Websites sections in the appendix. There are numerous resources for the do-it-yourself-er.

You should also turn to the same firms investment advisors use to hold their client's investments. We will cover these firms in the next chapter, but the discount brokerage firm often provides a "one-stop" shop with low costs, salaried brokers, and their websites often contain educational information you may find helpful. When I opened my Registered Investment Advisory Firm, I chose TD Ameritrade. TD Ameritrade, Fidelity, and Schwab are the big three. All of them also provide referrals to Registered Investment Advisors when you are ready to consider professional management.

You will not have difficulty finding information. The real problem for most people isn't finding it, it is getting through the massive quantity of it and finding what you need!

You might choose to start with the United States government. They offer a very good financial primer at http://www.usa.gov/Citizen/Topics/Money/Personal_Finance.shtml and on a related website, www.MyMoney.gov. Both sites have extensive information with links to free consumer guides.

The Industry and Investment Professionals

Even if you are a "do-it-yourself" investor, you will need a company to handle your account. For those investors who want to work with a professional, it can be difficult to decide which professional is best for your specific situation. Should you choose a broker, consultant, planner, or advisor? Maybe an agent or representative? Not to mention your attorney or accountant. Some of these professionals are affiliated with Wall Street and some are not.

Why did Wall Street create so many different types of financial services professionals? Although Wall Street created many different types of investment professionals, they were not alone. They had help! Every position on Wall Street was created to comply with regulations drafted by the US Congress in Washington, DC, or by regulatory agencies of the Federal Government.

The majority of the regulations affecting Wall Street were a direct result of the Great Depression. With the hope of preventing another economic disaster, the Federal and State governments created regulations and regulatory agencies to oversee the financial services industry. These regulations were not created in one day—they evolved over time and continue to evolve to this day. Major legislation was passed in 2010 that makes substantial changes to the financial services industry. Perhaps that is why one of the first things you learn when you join the financial services industry is, when it comes to the rules and regulations, change is a constant. Usually these changes are minor, but every decade or so, a major change should be anticipated.

You should be aware of the impact these regulations have on the delivery of investment products and services to investors. This section of the book is not comprehensive and is intended to help you gain a general understanding of the impact these regulations have on the firms, products, and professionals you may work with as an investor. Let's begin our conversation about financial professionals with a quick history of the regulators, and the regulations, that created them.

The Regulators

The financial services industry, as we know it today, has a wide number of regulatory agencies, investment firms, and types of professionals. As a result, there are many different types of financial professionals you may encounter in your search for the right advisor. You should know who regulates your advisor and what is legally required of them. This is not always easy to determine as financial regulations are not the same in every state and the laws regulating the industry are from multiple sources including the Federal Government, the States, and Self Regulatory Agencies. The appendix provides a list of the major regulators of the financial services industry with their websites. The following table provides a quick look of the regulators and their responsibilities.

Name (Year Established)	Level of Government	Responsibility
U.S. Treasury Department	Federal	Federal Gov't Finances, U.S. Economy, Safety, Soundness and Security of U.S. and International Financial Systems
Office of Thrift Supervision OTS (1831)	Federal	Savings and Loan Associations
Office of the Comptroller of the Currency OCC (1863)	Federal	All National Banks and Foreign Banks operating within the United States.
Federal Reserve Board FED (1913)	Federal	U.S. Monetary Policy and Banking Activities
Federal Deposit Insurance Corp FDIC (1933)	Federal	Federal and State Banks
Securities and Exchange Commission-SEC (1934)	Federal	Registered Investment Advisors and Investment Products
Commodity Futures Trading Commission-CFTC (1974)	Federal	All commodity futures and options contracts and dealers
Financial Industry Regulatory Authority-FINRA (2007)*	Self Regulatory Agency operating at the Federal Level	Broker Dealers and Registered Representatives
State Corporation Commission SCC (varies by state)	State	Business Registration, State Registered Investment Advisors, and Insurance Industry

All of these regulatory bodies are subject to the legislation enacted by Congress. The 111th Congress passed major legislation that may affect investors, regulators, and professionals. You do not need to read the regulations, memorize them, or become an expert on the existing or new legislation. You do need to recognize that almost every financial product, service, or professional was not arbitrarily created by the financial services industry. They are created to comply with a massive and comprehensive amount of related legislation. Most State's also have financial regulatory agencies, particularly those relating to insurance. The names of these organizations vary in each state and some states defer to the Federal Government. The state regulators are listed in the appendix.

The Firms

There are several different types of financial services firms. This section covers the type of firms you will most likely encounter in your search for the right advisor. The first type of firm we will discuss is the broker dealer and there are three basic types of broker-dealer firms: *full service, independent,* and *discount.* If you invest in any security, it is highly likely your account will be held at a broker dealer or at a custodian that conducts trades through a broker dealer.

Broker dealers primarily generate revenue by charging commissions for trades and through the sale of commission-based products including mutual funds and variable annuities. Broker dealers are currently subject to the suitability rule which require broker dealers to have reasonable grounds for believing any recommendation is suitable for their customer based upon the facts disclosed by the customer. The rule requires broker dealers to know the customer's financial status, tax status, investment objectives, and other information considered relevant by the broker dealer and registered representative. The suitability rule is extremely important and we will cover it in detail later in this chapter. The Financial Reform legislation passed by both houses of congress is a massive new legislative act which will affect the suitability rule. At the time of this writing, the final rules have not been drafted by the various agencies assigned this task by congress. Updates or links to regulatory and other market websites will be posted and maintained on the book's website, www.investiphobia.com.

Full service broker dealers are large firms and they engage in many financial activities other than securities transactions, such as financing corporations and managing investment portfolios. They maintain internal research departments and provide their registered representatives with buy and sell recommendations. Almost all full service firms are organized as publicly held companies and their stocks trade on the exchanges. They have branch offices and commission based registered representatives in most major cities. Full service firms also hold securities within their own firms and function as brokers, or agents, when selling securities they do not own and dealers, or principals, when they buy or sell securities for or from their own account. Full service firms have the largest internal staffs and, as a result, they generally charge the highest commissions for trades. Examples of full service firms include Morgan Stanley, UBS, and Raymond James.

Independent firms are similar to full service firms and the main difference between them is the structure of ownership. Independent does not mean they offer independent advice, rather it simply means they are not publicly traded companies. They may be held privately, owned by their employees, or subsidiaries of larger financial firms, often life insurance companies. Most independent firms have slightly lower commission schedules than their full service counterparts. This is partly because these firms often have minimal training programs and smaller, or sometimes no, internal research departments. Like their full service counterparts, independent firms often have branch offices and commission-based registered representatives in major cities across the United States. Examples of independent firms include LPL, Commonwealth, Edward Jones, Lincoln Financial Securities, and NYLIFE Securities.

Discount firms are able to offer lower trading commissions and fees because they rarely have internal research departments and fewer office locations than either full-service or independent firms. Many discount brokerage firms do not have offices at all and serve their clients by phone and on the Internet. These firms offer research provided by third parties like Standard and Poors, Morningstar, Value Line, and First Call. The two main operational differences that distinguish discount firms is they offer their services at a discount, hence the name, and their registered representatives are often, but not always, salaried employees. These firms also do not engage in as many financial activities as full service firms. This results in lower operating costs and they pass these lower expenses to their customers in the form of lower transaction fees. Although many registered representatives at discount firms are limited to taking and executing their client's securities trades, some of the discount brokers allow their representatives to recommend investments. Because the firms do not have internal research, their recommendations are based on the research conducted by third parties. This distinction is important because there is less potential for conflicts of interest. As an example, a full service firm may have a large inventory of a particular stock in its' own account. Their internal research department may be pressured to recommend this stock with the hope of selling it to their client base. This may be a conflict of interest because the brokerage firm has an incentive to recommend a particular stock to clients simply because they want to unload it from their own portfolio. This type of conflict is rare in the discount firm environment. Discount firms often function as custodians for another type of investment firm, the Registered Investment Advisor(RIA).

Registered Investment Advisors (RIA's)

Registered Investment Advisors provide investment advice or investment management and are primarily fee-only or fee-based. Fee-based advisors have the ability to serve their clients using fees or commissions. They can sell products. The Form ADV is available from the SEC website, www.sec.gov, and should be provided to you by your potential advisor. They should also disclose how they are compensated. Most private Registered Investment Advisors do not sell any products and are paid a fee for providing a service. These services include monitoring or managing your portfolio, preparing reports, and making recommendations or trading your account through a broker dealer or custodian. RIAs may provide money management either with discretion or without discretion. When they manage money with discretion, they have the authority to buy and sell investments in your account without prior notification to you. If they do not have discretion, they contact you in advance and obtain permission prior to making any trade. Registered investment advisory firms may charge their fees based on hourly rates, flat fees, a percentage of the assets that they manage, or a combination. Their fees must be disclosed to you and they are required to notify you on a regular basis of all fees you have paid them and how these fees were calculated. Your contract with an investment advisor spells out the specific types of fees that will be charged, the timing of the fees, and the method of calculating them. Most advisors debit these fees from your account so you do not have to write a check. RIAs are subject to the fiduciary standard. This requires RIAs to "act in the client's best interest". RIAs must avoid or disclose any conflicts of interest and provide services appropriate for their clients. RIAs may be large national firms or very small "solo" firms operated by one advisor. They are audited by either the state or the SEC depending on their size and the combination of Federal and State regulations for their home state. RIAs often serve wealthier clients exclusively and, as a result, their names may not be as familiar to you as other investment firms in this section. Most RIA firms are either Limited Liability Corporations(LLC) or corporations and they are generally owned by the professionals in the firm. The largest independent RIA firms include GenSpring Family Offices, LLC, Silvercrest Asset Management LLC, Rockefeller and Co, Inc., and Ronald Blue and Co, LLC. The vast majority of RIAs are small firms built around one or two individual advisors.

Generally, RIAs are registered with either the SEC or the state. Some RIA's are exempt from registration so it is important to verify the status of any RIA firm before hiring them. Non-Exempt RIA firms are required to file a Form ADV Parts I and II and a Schedule F each year. Among the information that these forms provide are a comprehensive overview of the firm, its ownership, types of services that it provides, the educational backgrounds of its owners, and the types of fees that it charges clients. If you meet with an RIA firm, you should request this form although many firms automatically provide it to you in your initial meeting.

Trust Companies

Trust companies are often departments of banks and they are regulated by a wide variety of regulators including the

Office of the Comptroller of the Currency. Trust companies are held to the fiduciary standard and must put the client's interest ahead of their own. When they are affiliated with a bank, the trust company functions as a completely separate business and must segregate all of its' client's assets from the bank. There are a significant number of private trust companies with no bank affiliation. These companies are still highly regulated and audited by Federal and State agencies. Among the services offered to individual investors by trust companies are money management, trust administration and estate settlement. They can pay bills for their clients and have custody of their client's assets. They often use outside and independent money managers with a dedicated team of professionals serving their clients. The team generally includes a relationship manager, a portfolio manager, an estate-planning specialist, and specialty employees who handle assets like real estate, collectibles, and small businesses. Trust companies often run businesses within estates until a buyer can be found. They have broad powers but are subject to numerous laws and audits performed by internal audit teams and by regulatory agencies.

Life Insurance Companies

Life insurance companies are currently regulated by the states for most products. The vast majority of the business handled by life insurance companies is not investment related, since they primarily provide life, health, disability, and long-term care insurance. They are included in this chapter because they often offer variable life and variable annuity policies. These products are generally commission-based and must be sold by registered representatives through their broker dealers. As mentioned earlier, many life insurance companies own independent broker dealers and their agents are often also registered representatives. Examples of life insurance companies include Northwestern Mutual, Mass Mutual, New York Life, and Prudential.

The People

You might have expected all financial professionals to have the same licenses, rules, and regulations before reading about all the regulators and types of investment firms. In reality, there are several significant and very different requirements of the four major types of people in the investment world. These differences include; type of registration and licensing, method of compensation, level of responsibility, method of handling clients, types of products recommended, and method of handling your accounts. It should come as no surprise that it is possible for one person to serve in different professional capacities, further complicating your ability to understand exactly what your professional is doing for you!

There are four basic types of financial services professionals and each is subject to a different set of regulations and oversight. They include brokers/registered representatives, registered investment advisors, insurance agents, and financial planners. You may also find attorneys and accountants who offer some, or all, of the services typically provided by financial services professionals either directly or through revenue sharing arrangements. This means you may work with attorneys or accountants who are themselves registered representatives and compensated by their broker dealer or paid directly by your broker. The following is a general overview of each type of professional and provides the basic information you will need to know before you work with any financial professional.

Brokers or Registered Representatives

Probably the most common financial professional is the registered representative, commonly known as a broker. This may surprise you, but by definition a broker (or registered representative) is registered to represent their broker dealer. They are paid on a commission basis for transactions they generate and for products they sell. Every broker dealer maintains a list of approved products and requires their brokers to sell only products from their specific broker dealer's list. However, these lists are not as limiting as they may sound because they usually contain a huge volume of products. It is important to consider the types of products rarely seen on the approved lists, no-load mutual funds. Because no-load funds do not pay any commission, it would be very rare to see any no-load fund on a broker dealers approved list. Broker dealers are responsible for training and supervising their registered representatives.

It is unusual to see the words *broker* or *registered representative* on a business card. The broker dealers usually allow their brokers to choose titles such as *Financial Advisor* instead. All brokers are regulated by FINRA and are described on FINRA's website as follows; brokers "who may also go by such generic titles as financial consultant, financial adviser, or investment consultant—are primarily securities salespeople." FINRA and the broker dealers supervise everything brokers are allowed to do, including the products they offer, the titles they use, their stationary and business cards, and what they can and cannot say in their communications with their prospects and clients.

It is important to remember that, as a result, brokers are transaction driven. Sales managers monitor the activity and sales trends of their brokers. Broker Dealers judge their brokers primarily on their ability to sell products or produce commissions on transactions. Free trips, bonuses, and other incentives are given to the best brokers based on the commissions they generate, which are called GDC, or gross dealer concession. Depending on the product, it can be difficult to know what your broker makes on a given transaction. If it is a managed product, like a mutual fund or variable annuity, then the GDC paid to the broker dealer is specified in a prospectus. The broker is required to provide the prospectus to all prospects, but these documents can be fifty pages or more, and the expense information may be difficult for the average person to understand. FINRA and other regulatory bodies are considering changes that will make the prospectus much easier for investors to read and understand.

Brokers are required to offer products that are "suitable" for you. Brokers are audited by their firms' internal compliance department as well as by regulators from the regulatory agencies, primarily FINRA. FINRA offers excellent information on its website, www.finra.org, regarding the brokerage industry, products, and the status of individual brokers through its "BrokerCheck" program.

Investment Advisory Representatives (IAR)

Investment Advisory Representatives own and/or work for Registered Investment Advisor Firms. The Investment Advisors Act of 1940 created these firms. They provide investment management and investment related services usually for a fee. They are not subject to the suitability rules of brokers and are held to the more stringent fiduciary standard. You should always verify that the investment advisor representative and the registered investment advisor are actually registered. Investment Advisor Representatives are people and they represent Registered Investment Advisors which are companies. People are not RIA's even when they are the sole owner of an RIA. People are IAR's representing RIA's which is even more confusing if they are handling your IRA!

Many of the firms that commit investment fraud are not actually registered at all. A simple check of the SEC website will verify whether they are actually a registered firm. You should also transfer funds, or write checks, only to the custodian or the firm itself. Never give money directly to a person affiliated with an advisor! You can obtain information on state and SEC registered investment advisors through the SEC's Investment Advisor Disclosure Database on their website, www.sec.gov under Investor Information or directly at http://www.adviserinfo.sec.gov/IAPD/Content/IapdMain/iapd_SiteMap.aspx. If you plan to meet with an investment advisor, you should review their Form ADV prior to the meeting. It will provide much of the information you need to know about the advisor. The SEC recently added information on the IAR to it's website. Regardless of the professional you choose, it is critical to verify their registration and compliance history.

Investment Advisors generally manage investments that are held at a separate custodian or discount brokerage firm. Some investment advisors have direct custody of your money and hold your account in their name. For investiphobic investors, choose a firm that does not have custody of your investment portfolio. Knowing your assets are held in your name with an independent and separate custodian is reassuring to most people who suffer from *investiphobia*.

Financial Planners

Financial planners provide assistance in developing and maintaining a written financial plan. They may be retained for a specific need, such as college planning, or for a comprehensive plan covering everything from your property and casualty insurance to your estate plan. Financial planners may charge by the hour, a flat rate, a retainer, or a percentage of the assets covered by the plan. They often have small, individually owned firms, although some work within a large planning firm. Many financial planners become certified financial planners, (CFP®), but this designation is not currently required for all planners. Most financial planners are also brokers, insurance agents, investment advisors, or accountants, and they are subject to the regulations for these services. As an example, a financial planner who is also a broker is still subject to oversight by their broker dealer and to regulations applying to the brokerage industry.

Financial planning is a relatively new field. For instance, the CFP® designation was first awarded in 1973. The field is growing, with over 126,000 CFP® certificants in the world and over 60,000 in the United States. This growth will probably ultimately result in the creation of a new regulator or the regulation of "pure" financial planners by an existing regulator. This does not mean you should not consider utilizing the services of a financial planner, as a matter of fact; financial planners are often very well-trained and able to work with a broad range of clients. Because they often charge hourly rates, you do not have to have a big investment portfolio to work with them. They can develop a budget, help you with property and casualty insurance, or help you to structure your debt. Many financial planners are also investment advisors.

Trust Officers

Trust officers work for trust companies. They usually service the wealthier clients, so they are generally more familiar with estate planning practices, as well as tax planning and trust administration. They can advise you on investing your assets, usually using a dedicated portfolio manager or by recommending third party investment professionals. They are trained to work with attorneys and accountants to coordinate asset allocation and tax planning strategies.

Because of their experience in administering trusts, a trust officer has a practical understanding of how these legal documents actually work. Some trust officers have investment management experience and training, but most have a dedicated portfolio manager that will actually manage the money.

Trust companies once had the reputation of using conservative money management methods, such as investing in high dividend blue chip stocks with the remainder in municipal or treasury bonds. Today, many trust companies use sophisticated investment management methods including commodities, hedge funds, and other alternative investments. Some of these changes are very good for investors, but the addition of complex investments to the trust companies portfolio requires investors to make sure that they understand where and how their money is invested. The fact that a hedge fund is held by your trust company does not change the fact that it is a hedge fund. It is important to remember that the FDIC does not cover the funds held by a trust company.

Trust companies can be a good choice for wealthy investors who have *investiphobia*. It is important to remember your relationship is with the trust company, not the trust officer. With the turnover in bank employees increasing, you should anticipate having different people assigned to your account.

Insurance Agents

Insurance agents are trained to provide products designed to protect you and your family from financial loss as a result of damages to your property, or your illness, disability, or death. These agents can assist you in obtaining life, health, long-term-care, and/or property and casualty insurance. Many life insurance agents may provide some level of estate planning, often in conjunction with an attorney or accountant. The State Insurance Commission of their home state and any state where they wish to sell insurance licenses most insurance agents to conduct business. If they offer variable annuities or variable life insurance, then they also are registered representatives because all variable products are investment securities. You can obtain information about an agent through your state's website. These listings are shown on the National Association of Insurance Commissioners website, www.naic.org. The NAIC also provides several excellent consumer guides which may be downloaded or requested through their website. These include guides to life insurance, fixed annuities, long-term-care insurance, as well as property and casualty insurance. Unlike the securities industry, which offers many "no load" products, insurance is still primarily a commission based, or load, product. Many products do not exist in a "no-load" form. Hopefully the day will come when the full array of insurance products is available in "no-load" versions with the savings going directly to the customer.

Accountants

Accountants are trained primarily as auditors or tax preparers and many of them are Certified Public Accountants (CPA). Some CPAs continue their training to become personal financial specialists (PFS). This extra certification is an indication that the CPA plans to work with clients beyond the more typical tax preparation or audit role. Both the CPA and PFS are obtained by passing an exam provided by the American Institute of Certified Public Accountants (AICPA).

By law, CPAs are fiduciaries. Like investment advisors, they must serve their clients' needs ahead of their own. Accountants may also be registered representatives of a broker dealer. The work they offer as registered representatives is not subject to the fiduciary standard.

Attorneys

Attorneys are fiduciaries and are required to represent your interests. Attorneys may also pursue additional certifications or advanced degrees such as the LLM (Master of Laws) degree with a specialty in taxation, indicating substantial training in tax planning and preparation. In some states, attorneys may also be registered representatives. They are not subject to the fiduciary standard when providing services as a registered representative.

You should retain an attorney to handle the drafting of your will and your estate documents. They should also be a member of your advisory team, along with your main advisor and your accountant. An attorney can also serve as your trustee and executor. Many people name a family member to serve in a co-executor or co-trustee capacity to make sure the family is involved in the decision-making process even after you have passed away. We live in a country that is based on the rule of law, and attorneys are often our best legal representatives.

A good attorney may be your, and your family's, best protection against the many investment- and non-investment-related issues that can negatively affect your portfolio and your legacy.

Professional Designations

Financial professionals need to stay abreast of the most recent developments in the markets, investment vehicles, regulations, research, and the most appropriate ways to allocate your assets. Some designations, require their certificants to complete continuing education to maintain their designation. This is beneficial for both the professional and their clients. By staying up-to-date, professionals maintain their existing knowledge and also become more proficient in meeting your financial needs. You may encounter many different designations in your search for the right advisor. Ask your advisor about their designations, why they chose them, and what each designation requires. You will gain insight into your professional and their own objectives, but most importantly, you will know whether a particular professional has the training and certification to work with you. There are a massive number of designations today and FINRA maintains a list of these on their website. The following list is not comprehensive and includes common, reputable, and significant, designations you should know. They include:

Chartered Financial Analyst, CFA

The CFA curriculum is a rigorous, intensive, and lengthy program intended to assure proficiency in analyzing corporate and municipal securities; as well as assuring proficiency in managing investment portfolios. This designation is accepted throughout the world. Candidates must complete three distinctive and extensive areas of study integrating economics, statistics, accounting, and investments. Each area of study requires the passing of a six-hour exam. This designation is awarded by the Institute of Chartered Financial Analysts. CFA designees are "encouraged" to complete recertification.

Certified Investment Management Analyst, CIMA

The CIMA curriculum is very similar to the particular CFA area of study devoted to managing investment portfolios. This designation is awarded by the Investment Management Consultants Institute. The CIMA program prepares a financial professional to evaluate the proficiency and performance of investment managers. CIMA's are usually retained by pension funds, foundations and endowments to assist in selecting investment managers appropriate for their respective investing objectives. To achieve this designation candidates are required to complete a one-year self-study program, attend an intensive week- long session at a designated university business school, and pass a four-hour examination.

Chartered Life Underwriter, CLU

The CLU designation is held by financial professionals specializing in wealth and estate protection through insurance and annuity contracts. It is a most respected designation within the life insurance industry, and one of the oldest professional designations among financial professionals. The required curriculum requires the successful completion of eight intensive courses administered by the American College in Bryn Mawr, Pennsylvania.

Chartered Financial Consultant, ChFC

The ChFC designation is also granted by the American College. Some consider it an enhancement of the CLU program, because it focuses on lifetime wealth planning issues other than income assurance and estate planning. In addition to the eight courses required for the CLU designation, ChFC candidates must take four other courses focusing on tax planning, investment strategies, retirement planning, and education funding.

Certified Financial Planner, CFP

The curriculum covers a comprehensive body of knowledge extensively covering financial planning topics. Upon successfully completing all of the courses, candidates are then required to pass two rigorous five-hour examinations. The CFP is the most widely recognized certification among financial professionals and it is not an easy designation to obtain. CFP certificants have shown their dedication to their profession by obtaining and maintaining the CFP designation. The program is governed by the Certified Financial Planner Board of Standards in Washington, D. C.

Registered Life Planner, RLP

The Kinder Institute of Life Planning (Littleton, MA) provides workshops, intensive trainings and consulting services to financial advisors worldwide. In its own words: *"the Institute focuses on the human side of financial planning. In Life Planning we discover a client's deepest and most profound goals through a process in structured and non-judgmental inquiry. Then, using a mix of professional and advanced relationship skills, we inspire clients to pursue their aspirations, discuss and resolve obstacles, create a concrete financial plan, and provide ongoing guidance..."*

Candidates for the RLP designation must a complete a 3-part seven-month curriculum dedicated to developing the counseling and relationship skills advocated by the Institute.

Enrolled Agent, (EA)

An EA is a federally-authorized tax practitioner. This designation is a license, not a designation. The license is earned in one of two ways, by passing a comprehensive examination which covers all aspects of United States tax code; or by having worked at the IRS for five years in a position which regularly interpreted and applied the tax code and its regulations. "Enrolled" means to be licensed to practice by the federal government, and "Agent" means authorized to appear in the place of the taxpayer before the IRS. Only EAs, Certified Public Accountants, and attorneys can represent a taxpayer before the IRS.

Methods of Compensation

Now that you know the regulations, the firms, and the professionals, it is important to consider the various methods of compensation. It is highly unlikely the firm or professional who handles your account is not compensated, even if you use a low-costs discount firm! Most investment firms and professionals are paid either by commission, fees, or a combination of both.

Commission

Commissions are paid for the sale of a product, like a mutual fund or variable annuity. You will also pay commissions for transactions involving individual securities, exchange traded funds, and other securities which trade on any exchange. The professionals who handle the sale, or transaction, of investment products are licensed as brokers. Insurance agents are also compensated by commission.

Fee-Base and Fee-Only

Fees may be assessed by advisors who are investment advisory representatives of a Registered Investment Advisor. Some of these firms, and professionals, are compensated purely by fees and do not receive commissions, They are referred to by the term, "fee-only". Some firms, and professionals, function as both a broker-dealer or broker/registered representative and as an advisor. These professionals are compensated depending on what they provide to their clients. If they function as a broker/registered representative, they are paid a commission for the sale or transaction. When functioning as an advisor, they are paid a fee. We refer to these professionals as "fee-based".

The right advisor for you may be compensated by commission, fee-only, or fee-based professional. It is important for you to know how your professional is compensated.

The Suitability Rule versus The Fiduciary Standard

It is important for investors to consider the differences between the suitability rule and the fiduciary standard. Under current regulations, brokers are subject to the suitability rule and investment advisors are subject to the fiduciary standard. The suitability rule requires brokers and their broker dealers to have reasonable grounds for believing any recommendation is suitable for their customer based upon the facts disclosed by the customer. The rule requires broker dealers to have the customer's financial status, tax status, investment objectives, and other information considered relevant by the broker dealer and registered representative. The term "investment advisor representative" is more than a job title and, from a legal perspective, all investment advisors are held to the fiduciary standard. A fiduciary is one who must act in another's interest, rather than in their own interests. Investment advisors are required to go beyond the information disclosed by their client to make sure their recommendations are in the clients' best interests. Unlike brokers, who must provide "suitable" products, investment advisors must provide "appropriate" services and recommendations. The following story illustrates the difference between the "suitability" and "appropriateness" standards.

On a very hot day, a thirsty person is given a glass of ice-cold lemonade to quench his thirst. Unfortunately, he is a Type-1 diabetic and the heavily sweetened lemonade causes him to go into shock. The lemonade provider did not know their customer was diabetic. Since lemonade is certainly a suitable thirst quencher for thirsty people on a hot day, it satisfies the "suitability" rule. The suitability rule does not require the provider of any service to treat their client as a unique individual. The suitability rule is a general rule, applying to groups of similar investors as opposed to the specific investor. If the lemonade provider was held to a fiduciary standard, they should have acted in the client's interest. Clearly, the lemonade was suitable, but not "appropriate", for this specific customer.

Brokers and advisors are regulated, but the rules are different. Don Trone describes the suitability and fiduciary rules in his book, *Fiduciary Ethos*. Don is no stranger to the debate. He has dedicated his career to defining the fiduciary standard and testified before a US Senate Finance Committee in 2007. Don believes all clients deserve a measurable standard of care from their financial professional, but he also believes it is acceptable and appropriate for there to be more than one standard. All standards of care should have in common doing what is best for the client. If there are different standards, then it is important that the applicable standard of care is known and agreed to by both the client and the professional involved. The chart below is from Don's book, *Fiduciary Ethos*:

You may choose to use a broker or an advisor based on your unique circumstances and needs. If you choose to use a broker, you are responsible for making sure the investments chosen are appropriate for you. You may consider the do-it-yourself approach and use a discount brokerage firm. Many offer tools and access to no-load mutual funds and low transaction costs. They often also pay their internal brokers a salary with a bonus package instead of a commission. This means less pressure to push any given product, which makes these firms a rational choice for investors who cannot find an advisor in their area, or who prefer to do-it-themselves. RIAs use discount brokers, or bank custodians, to hold their client's funds. It makes sense for those who either decide on the do-it-yourself approach or who have insufficient funds for advisors to consider discount brokerage firms, like TD Ameritrade, Fidelity, or Schwab—or no-load mutual fund companies like Vanguard, T. Rowe Price, and Fidelity.

Summary

Among the professionals in the finance industry, the most common investment professionals you are most likely to encounter are brokers, investment advisor representatives, financial planners, and insurance agents. Attorneys and accountants may offer similar services or be licensed as an investment professional. Many professionals choose to wear multiple hats. When they are playing more than one role, it can be difficult to know precisely what capacity your professional is in when they work with you. The following questions might illustrate the difficulties in this situation:

> What is the primary responsibility of a broker who is also an investment advisor? Or an accountant who is licensed as a broker and as an insurance agent? What if your CFP is a broker? Is that the same as a CFP who is an investment advisor? What if your advisor pays your accountant ongoing fees in a revenue sharing relationship? Does that affect your accountant's independent advice?

In my opinion, investors should always assume the professional with multiple hats is in the least-responsible position. Given a choice of owning or denying fiduciary responsibility, most professionals would choose the position with the least liability. In these circumstances, it is your responsibility to make sure your investments are appropriately handled. There is nothing wrong with having your account handled by a full-service broker. If you prefer owning individual stocks, the research available to full-service brokers could make them your best choice. This is also true for investors who want to work with a local professional but whose portfolio is too small for advisors and planners. The main point of this chapter is investors should be sufficiently informed about their professionals liability and method of compensation. It is a matter of personal choice, based on full disclosure and your personal goals and objectives. There are good people in the industry who are available to help you as brokers, advisors, planners, agents, attorneys and accountants.

Finally, remember to verify your professional's licensing and credentials. You can determine whether a financial professional is registered by visiting the sites of FINRA, the SEC, or your state financial regulatory agency. If you cannot ascertain the registration of a person purporting to give you financial advice, simply do not do business with that person.

The Risk Profile Questionaire or New Account Form

In your initial meeting with most financial professionals, you will probably be asked to complete some sort of questionnaire. Generally, this document will ask questions about your current financial situation, investment experience, time horizon and investment objectives, liquidity needs, and acceptable level of investment risks. Financial planners will include your property and casualty insurance, budget, cash flow, and all aspects of your personal finances. In this section of the book, we will look at each section of a basic questionnaire and examine its purpose. We will look at the perceived purpose of the questionnaire from both the investor's perspective and that of the financial professional.

The first section of the questionnaire is usually about your current financial situation. It will include questions on the type of investments you currently hold and will also ask if you have ever held other investments. As an example, your current portfolio might contain certificates of deposit, individual stocks, and mutual funds. You may also indicate that although you do not currently own a variable annuity or stock options, you have used them in the past. You will also probably get a question about your current income and your tax bracket. The purpose of these questions is to show your investment professional what you have done in the past. It also provides a snapshot of your current investment portfolio and your income level.

In the investment experience section, you will be asked to indicate the level of experience and knowledge that you have as an investor. There are many different ways that these questionnaires determine your experience. They may ask you to choose among the designations "beginner," "experienced," and "expert," or they may ask you to indicate how many years you have been investing. They may ask you about your comfort level in handling your investment portfolio. In any case, the purpose of this section is to allow the brokerage firm or advisor to document your experience level.

The next section covers the account that you are planning to establish. You will be asked about the time horizon and objective for the account. For instance, you might indicate that you plan to retire in five to seven years and that you would like the account to grow during that time period. The purpose of this section is to begin the process of determining how you would like the account invested.

You will be asked about your intention to deposit or withdraw additional funds and whether you have any anticipated liquidity needs. Liquidity, in this case, means the amount of money that you need to have accessible and the amount that you already know you will need at a point within the time horizon of the account. You might indicate that you plan to make additional deposits, the amount of the deposits, and that you plan to buy a car next year for $20,000.

Most questionnaires also have a section to determine your comfort level with fluctuations in your account value. You might be asked to provide the maximum loss you can tolerate in a given year or what you would do if your account lost 20 percent of its value. This lets your professional document the appropriate investments that are acceptable for your account. If you indicate you cannot tolerate a loss, the account will need to be limited to investments that are guaranteed. If you indicate losses are not an issue, then an aggressive growth objective could be established.

From an investor perspective, the purpose of this document is to provide a process that will help your investment professional design a portfolio that is right for you. You hope that they can handle your investments in a way that meets your objectives and that they will generate the target return with no unacceptable losses. They take the time to answer their questions and discuss your needs. You will feel better that your professional knows what you want. This is also the reason that most professionals use questionnaires or cover this information in the initial meeting.

In my opinion, the commission brokerage industry views the new account form, or risk questionnaire, differently. Many professionals are trained to believe that the purpose and use of the questionnaire is to put them in the driver's seat as they assist you in completing the form, and that completing the form will protect them from liability. Numerous seminars and articles in professional journals point to the questionnaire as the best way for an investment professional to document their files and protect themselves from investor liability. In laymen's terms, the questionnaire may not be about you at all—for some professionals, it is all about them. For these professionals, if you have completed the form and they have selected products that are suitable for you, based on your answers, then they have done an acceptable job of handling your account. They have made you happy and are protected from a liability standpoint. Note that your investment situation may actually be worse as a result, but, for at least a little while, you will be happier.

The mismatch in expectations of the investors and professionals is the root problem with the questionnaire. You may want to talk about the things that are important to you and how you need help finding a way to support your lifestyle. The questionnaire is designed to document whether you are a growth or an income investor. There is no box or blank for information about the garden you are growing to help feed the poor, or the year you would like to spend in Europe, or whatever drove you to get professional investment help in the first place. The questionnaire, whether it is incorporated into the new account form or presented as a completely separate document, pulls the investor into a process that is oriented toward product sales. It is not substantial enough to even begin to address the things that may be important to you as an investor. It puts a highly-trained securities salesperson in the driver's seat. Answering these questions feels similar to filling out your first loan or job application. You may even be hoping that the brokerage firm will approve your application!

Let's contrast the investment profile questionnaire with a similar questionnaire used by doctors. When you go to a new doctor, you will complete a questionnaire that provides the doctor with your name, contact information, insurance information, medical history, drug allergies, and current symptoms. You complete the questionnaire so that the doctor can treat you and give you what you need to be well again. The doctor is probably not in the room when you fill out the questionnaire. It is given to you by the receptionist before your appointment.

The doctor—or, often, a nurse practitioner—reviews the information to learn about your medical history to determine your current state of health. Admittedly, the form also provides documentation that helps protect the doctor from liability, but the form does not put the doctor in the driver's seat. It does not begin a process of selecting the medical products that he will be compensated for selling you. The doctor is probably not hoping you will help qualify them for an all-inclusive trip to Jamaica. Once you meet with the doctor, she may ask questions to clarify or new questions to help him find out how he can help you find the treatment that you need.

In medicine, the patient wants the doctor to determine if she needs any treatment, and, if so, to provide the treatment that she needs. The doctor wants to examine her and provide the treatment that she needs. The relationship works because both the doctor and the patient want the same outcome. When it comes to investing, most investors want an investment professional who will give them what they want. The broker wants to know what the investor wants so that the broker can satisfy the client and efficiently make a new sale. The relationship appears to work because both want the same outcome. So what's the problem?

In my experience, investors come to professionals because of what they want, but they really want the professional to provide what they need. Although this is a perfect setup for the investment sales representative, it creates a dilemma for a good investment advisor or financial planner. It takes courage for any professional to tell a prospective client that what they want is not what they need. By confronting a prospect or by helping them confront themselves, the professional risks losing the new client and, quite frankly, they also risk irritating the customer. Because investment advisors are fiduciaries, they often must accept the challenge of communicating the differences between a new client's wants and what they actually need.

How do we eliminate the mismatch of expectations and address the real investment issues that are so often lost in the process? We have to establish a level of trust. Both you and your advisor will have to earn it from each other. Trust is critical in the relationship between clients and their advisors. It takes time to develop, but it is well worth it. When the relationship is handled properly, both parties benefit in both the long run and the short term. Your part is really not that difficult. If you want an advisor to give you sound advice and to address your needs, you simply need to tell them what you want while understanding and expecting them to tell you if your wants do not match your needs. You should also require them to back up their recommendations with understandable explanations.

We do not need a new tool, product, or method—we simply need advisors and investors to handle the current questionnaire in a better way. Generally speaking, the best advisors use the questionnaire as a part of a process to get to know you and your financial situation so that they can determine what you need. They can do it easily with your permission. One thing that may help is if you use a questionnaire to get to know them, too!

When you use your questionnaire to get to know your potential advisor, please remember that almost all investment professionals are not only competent communicators but have also received training on the best ways to sell ideas and communicate with their clients. An experienced professional has probably heard most of the typical questions that an investor might ask, and they are trained and prepared to answer them. You may be a great communicator yourself and may have no difficulty asking a new potential professional the questions that you need answered to help you determine if they are the right advisor for you. But if, for whatever reason, you feel uncomfortable, it is important to remember that the person across the table is trained to make you feel at ease! Ask away, and do not be afraid to move on to another advisor if you are not happy with his answers, style, or personality.

Once you and your advisor have gathered the necessary knowledge, your advisor should use the information that you have given them to create an Investment Policy Statement(IPS). The use of the IPS can be one of the *best* cures for almost all the forms of *investiphobia*! Although the advisor should prepare the initial draft of the document, they will need you to help them make sure that it accurately represents the goals and expectations that each of you have for your portfolio.

The IPS documents a substantial amount of information about how your investments will be managed. You and your advisor should work together to draft an IPS that accurately documents:

1) Assets included and excluded in the IPS
2) Statement of Objectives
3) Risk Tolerance
4) Time Horizon
5) Modeled Return
6) Modeled Loss
7) Asset Classes Included and Excluded
8) Asset Allocation (Target with range above and below)
9) Type of Investment Authorized (Individual Securities, Mutual Funds, ETFs, etc.)
10) Duties and Responsibilities of:
    i) Investment Advisor
    ii) Investment Managers
    iii) Custodian

11) Selection Criteria for Investment Managers
12) Control Procedures
    i) Rebalancing
    ii) Criteria for Firing Investment Managers
    iii) Monitoring Costs

FI360, located in Pittsburgh, is an organization dedicated to investment fiduciary education, practice management, and support that has established them as the go-to source of investment fiduciary insights. A sample of their IPS is available as a free download from their website, www.fi360.com. Your IPS does not have to be identical or even in the same format, but it should include the same information.

There is a feeling of security that comes from accurate and detailed documentation. The IPS provides your advisor with the instructions they need to handle your account. It also provides you with a method to measure your advisor. Working together with your advisor, to create this document, is one of the best ways to make sure you both are working towards the same destination. This document should be reviewed annually or when your circumstances change. It is designed to support a long-term investment period and should not change as a result of market movement! On the contrary, it should provide comfort during market downturns because you and your advisor have documented how to handle the account in every market condition!

How to Find and Choose the Right Advisor

This is the most important chapter in the book. The information it contains will be helpful to you as you look for a competent and knowledgeable professional to assist you in the management of your portfolio. This chapter is also written about a topic heavily addressed on the web, magazine and newspaper articles, television shows, and other books.

What source gives us the best information? Well, some of the material designed to help you choose an advisor is similar to material we often receive that helps us choose a president. In other words, organizations such as the Financial Planning Association (FPA) or the National Association of Professional Financial Advisors (NAPFA) produce pamphlets or brochures supporting the CFP designation. Others are produced by brokerage firms such as Raymond James or Merrill Lynch to promote brokers and advisors affiliated with their firm. Still others are produced by mutual fund companies such as Fidelity and Vanguard. All may have good suggestions, but you should consider the source in relation to the advice offered. As an example of an appropriate disclosure you should consider in relation to the advice offered by this book, the author is an investment advisor representative and a licensed insurance agent.

The legal configuration of the fee-only registered investment advisor is the one best suited for most investors. But, there are very valid reasons for professionals to choose the brokerage or agent configuration. As an example, even though there are no-load, or non-commission, insurance products available in the marketplace, when it comes to the insurance industry, only a very small percentage of companies offer an even smaller array of commission-free products. Basically, if you want John Hancock long-term care coverage or a Mass Mutual universal life policy, someone is going to be paid a commission. An agent may choose, but is not required, to disclose the commission in advance so that their client is aware of all compensation issues. In many states, regulations forbid any refund or sharing of insurance commissions with the client or any non-licensed entity. It is not perfect, but until the no-load insurance companies offer the level of products available on a commission basis, it is understandable that trustworthy professionals may choose to be commission-based agents. The agent should never charge both a fee and a commission.

There are also legitimate reasons for a professional to choose to serve their clients as a broker. The brokerage industry is an easier environment for professionals who handle clients in the accumulation stage who are typically young and have smaller investment accounts. Wealthy do-it-yourselfers often choose full-service brokers because they believe the research capabilities of these firms gives them more value than the extra costs of higher commission rates. Who you choose, and why your financial services professional chose their specific configuration, are questions only you, the investor, and your financial services professional can answer. There is nothing inherently wrong with choosing any of the different types of financial professionals to handle your account. It is critical, however, that your financial professional demonstrates their commitment to doing what is in your best interest. It is also critical you accept and trust in their commitment, while periodically very verifying their actions and recommendations.

Ultimately, no matter who you choose, you are the boss! Make sure your advisor is comfortable and understands their role in your investment life.

This chapter describes the various criteria you should consider in evaluating an advisor. There is an advisor questionnaire in the appendix, including a section of questions that cover each of these criteria.

Designations or Certifications

Many of the articles that answer the "How do I find a good advisor?" question indicate that the designations and certifications a professional has obtained are the most important criteria in choosing an advisor. An advisor or planner's certifications are certainly something you should consider; however, they are not the most important factors. They are the first criteria listed in this book, because they are the least important in choosing an advisor!

When you go to a new doctor, you know they passed medical school and received their MD or they would not be able to practice medicine. For most people, there are only two relevant questions to ask when selecting a doctor, and neither question is directed at the doctor! The first question, "Is the doctor accepting new patients?" is normally directed at the receptionist. The second is, "Is the doctor still in my insurance company's network of providers?" and you probably will not ask the doctor this question, either! When the doctor walks in, they will ask the questions and they have earned the right by passing one of the hardest training regimens in the world. Even with the regulation and standards of the medical profession, not all MD's are competent. But all doctors must pass a similar program before they can practice medicine. The program is very difficult and requires years.

To practice law, attorneys must obtain the Juris Doctor (JD) degree and pass the state bar exam. Doctors must obtain the Medical Doctor (MD) degree and fulfill their residency requirements before they can be licensed to practice medicine. Neither the JD nor the MD is a designation; both are doctoral degrees.

In the financial industry, there is no equivalent to the JD or MD. There are academic degrees in finance, including the Masters in Financial Services, that show academic training but there are no required degrees that are required to work in the financial services field. Financial designations are indications that the individual has studied a specific volume of material to gain the academic knowledge of the subject covered. But unlike law, medicine, and accounting, there is no required designation, or academic degree, to be in the financial services industry. There are required licenses in the insurance and investment fields, but many of these licenses indicate that the recipient achieved a score of 70 percent or higher on one or more multiple choice exams! A registered representative can sell products after just two of these pass/fail exams!

There are so many designations available today that only a sample of them is covered within this book. The FINRA website, www.finra.com, keeps an up-to-date designation list, and you should go to their website if you are unsure of the meaning of the acronym that follows any professional's name.

It is appropriate to consider the designations held by any professional, but it is not a valid criterion by which to include or exclude an advisor! The designations should be considered because they indicate a commitment on the part of the professional, provide them with specialized training, and the primary designations included in this section are not easy to obtain!

Designations can be misleading when it comes to the professionals' sense of fiduciary responsibility to their clients. One of the most popular and widely held designations is the CFP. This designation has existed for over thirty years and is considered by many to be the industry standard. CFP certificants must comply with the CFP Code of Conduct, which has been updated several times since the designation was created. As a matter of fact, the CFP Board recently updated its Code of

Conduct for practitioners and strengthened its commitment to holding all CFP certificants to put their client's interest first.

One could easily assume that any CFP who is working with a client is held to a fiduciary standard for all of the work they do with their client. However, upon closer examination, the CFP is only held to a fiduciary standard when actually performing financial planning. When a CFP sells a mutual fund and is paid a commission, they are functioning as a registered representative. In that capacity, their obligation is to their employer, not to their client. In essence, a registered representative who is also a CFP certificant is not a fiduciary when they provide a product. They are only a fiduciary when they provide financial planning services. The Code of Conduct does indicate that the CFP certificant must still behave in a professional manner and never do anything that is not in the interest of the client. Until the CFP Board decides and enforces a continuous fiduciary requirement, you should not assume that the CFP is acting in a fiduciary capacity if they are also a registered representative.

In addition, registered representatives must have all of their work approved by their broker dealer. They cannot perform independent planning and accept a fiduciary duty without approval by their broker dealer. Broker dealers are liable for the actions of their registered representative, and therefore they are highly unlikely to allow independent financial planning. As a result, most planners who are registered representatives use a boilerplate computer-planning program approved by their broker dealer. If you want an approach designed specifically for your unique circumstances, then a broker dealer's boilerplate software program is probably not the best place to start.

The CFP is a prestigious certification, but it is the method of compensation that determines the true value the CFP certificant offers their clients. If designations are important to you, include them in your criteria, but give more weight to each of the other criteria covered in this chapter. If the CFP designation is important to you, and you want someone in a fiduciary capacity, then you should work with one of the many CFP's that are in the National Association of Personal Financial Planners. These CFP's have a very strong code of ethics and are almost always affiliated with a registered investment advisor.

You should also review any odd designations that are completely new to you. If you do not recognize the designation, you should ask the professional what the designation means, what they did to obtain it, and why they chose it. If it still does not make sense to you, then you should not work with them!

To the extent that you consider designations, consider professionals with the CFP, CLU, ChFC, CIMA or CFA. All of these designations are established in the industry and are strong indications of professionals committed to their profession. They also require, or encourage in the case of the CFA designation, their certificants to complete continuing education to maintain their status. These five designations all have a long history, in comparison to other designations, and they also are the most common designations that you may encounter. You might also consider the Registered Life Planner (RLP) as an excellent designation for the advisor to an investiphobe! As discussed previously, the RLP includes the human element which is important for investors who would like to invest without fear!

In conclusion, consider the designations held by the professional, but keep it in perspective. There is no MD or JD or CPA when it comes to financial planning and investment management.

Education

The educational background of the professional should be considered when selecting your advisor. Like the certifications in the previous section, the educational background of your prospective advisor is important, but not critical. Unlike law, medicine, and accounting, the financial services industry does not have a required major or area of study. This may be due to the fact the financial services industry is still evolving and many people in the industry began as bankers, brokers, realtors, and the like.

You may discover that many of your prospective advisors did not major in business. You also may find those with a liberal arts background often do not use the jargon that is the domain of the business, finance, and economics majors. Sovran Bank, a predecessor bank of Bank of America, hired liberal arts majors because they wanted people who worked with clients to be good communicators. They felt it was easier to equip the liberal arts major with financial knowledge than to teach a business major to speak using common terms. Obviously, this did not apply to the commercial areas of the bank, where specific financial knowledge was required, but it makes sense when you think about the fact that most retail, trust, and investment clients are not business majors.

An advisor's educational history is important to discuss in your initial meeting. If nothing else, the discussion will reveal a great deal about the advisor's background and interests. It also may lead to the more important criteria you should consider. As an example, when discussing college and postgraduate work, the professional will be remembering those first years of independence we all remember experiencing after graduating from high school. Without having to ask, you will know where they lived for four years, their favorite college team, and some of the activities they enjoyed in college.

After all, you want the advisor to talk at the beginning of the appointment so you can get to know them. A good advisor knows they need to lead at the beginning and getting to know you is extremely important. By talking about their own personal background, they hope to make you comfortable enough to reveal your information to them. If they are really good, they will spend most of the rest of the appointment listening to you! If they are outstanding, you won't notice how they accomplish this. If they majored in a subject that does not appear to be related to investments or financial planning, the door is open for you to ask them how they found their way into the financial industry.

A discussion of an advisor's educational background almost always lead to a discussion of the first very important factor in choosing an advisor: experience.

Experience

Although a young professional may be well-trained and may even hold a prestigious designation, you may want to consider your needs before hiring them. If they do not have several years of experience, then the designations and educational background previously covered should be given more weight in your decision process. If you are mainly concerned with budgeting, education, insurance, building wealth, or tax planning, then it is certainly appropriate to consider a young planner who has a solid education and certification. It may also be very appropriate if you are also young!

If you have already grown or inherited a substantial portfolio, if you are retired or nearing retirement, and if your primary need is investment management, then you should find an advisor with more than ten years of experience. Given the investment climate of 2000-2002 and from 2008 – 2009, any professional who has been in the field for ten years has experience in the bull market of 2004-2007 and at least two bear markets! If you suffer from any form of *investiphobia*, a little gray hair adorning the head of your advisor can be comforting in a difficult market. Advisors with grey hair were once young and resented the experienced advisors when they seemed to effortlessly win wealthier clients. But, if they are honest with themselves, they know that almost all professionals began with smaller accounts until they gained the confidence and knowledge to be comfortable working with wealthier clients.

As you review your prospective advisor's experience, you should look for the experience directly related to their practice and make note of how it relates to your situation. In addition, you should not ignore the life experience they may have gained while working in other fields. Many financial professionals did not go directly from college to the financial industry. If a prospective planner has worked in a store, managed a coffee shop, taught school, or been a merchant marine, they may have a better understanding of your life and work. They may have once been on your side of the table, quite literally, and needed professional help with their budget, insurance, or portfolio. This experience may have been their inspiration for becoming a planner or advisor. Depending on how their "other" career experiences relate to you, you should consider placing as much value on that experience as you do on their financial experience. They still should have at least ten years in the financial services industry, particularly when investing is your primary need.

Experience is a very important consideration when selecting an advisor. It is important to remember you are the only one who can determine if they have enough experience for you to be comfortable and confident enough to let them assist you with your finances. If you do not feel the advisor has enough experience, you do not need to continue evaluating them. Experience is the first of the criteria that is important enough to veto hiring the advisor. This is also true for each of the remaining criteria. If you are uncomfortable with the advisor's performance on this or any single one of the following criteria, do not hire the advisor. Continue your search until you find one that has enough experience as well as the following characteristics.

Compensation

There are several ways a financial professional can be compensated for the services they provide to you. Because of the huge number of brokers, the charging of commissions is probably the most common type of compensation. The number of fee-only planners and advisors is increasing, but the brokerage industry is still the majority of the market. As mentioned earlier, if you have *investiphobia*, then you should be careful when working with any professional earning the majority of their income from commissions on investment sales. When a financial professional relies on commissions, they are more likely to be transaction-oriented. This can result in a continuous need to change investments to generate commission income. It can also bring products with lengthy surrender periods and high annual expenses into your portfolio. It is more difficult, sometimes impossible, to know exactly what you are paying when you use a commission-based professional. Commission-based mutual funds not only have either front or back end loads; they also may have higher ongoing expenses when compared to no load or advisor class funds. Sometimes these more expensive funds are available without a load through an advisor. But, the choice of a professional is a decision that is yours and yours alone. There are many excellent brokers who do a very good job for their clients. Do not hesitate to use a broker if they pass all of your criteria.

As previously discussed, the "no load" offerings in the insurance industry are not as viable an option. It is difficult to find any no-load life insurance, with the exception of a very few whole life products, with a guaranteed death benefit! For the commission products, it is important to note that insurance commissions are not negotiable. There are regulations that prevent an agent from refunding or reducing the commission, and the punishment for violation is severe. Have an attorney, a knowledgeable planner, or an accountant assist you in determining your need for insurance and ask them to review the policy prior to purchase.

Financial planners also may charge a fee for assisting you in locating insurance products, but even if they are members of NAPFA, they will often assist you in buying the policy through a commission-based insurance agent. When working with an attorney, accountant, or financial planner on insurance, you need to ask them to specify their relationship with the insurance agent. Make sure any compensation sharing arrangements or solicitation fees are fully disclosed. Full disclosure occurs when you know, in advance and in writing, the specific dollar amount or percentage of commission that will be shared. You should not have to ask for this information. If your advisor does not give it willingly, or refuses to provide it in writing, then you need to find another advisor. Remember, attorneys and accountants are often in these fee or commission sharing arrangements.

Many accountants are becoming agents and brokers and also receive commission compensation. You need to know that their "independent" fee-only recommendation is not in addition to a solicitor's fee or commission paid by the insurance agent or company. If you decide to purchase insurance from an agent recommended by a fee-only planner or accountant, ask both of them to sign a document indicating that the commission is not being split, that no solicitor's fee is being paid, and that the agent is not compensating the referring planner or accountant in any way. Otherwise, that "independent" fee-only advice may not be as independent as it seems.

When you are working with a financial planner or an investment advisor in any area other than insurance, you should look for an advisor who allows you to pay your fee directly from your accounts. Their fees are typically calculated and charged based on one of the following three methods: hourly, flat, or percentage-based.

Financial planners often charge an hourly fee or a flat fee to prepare a comprehensive financial plan. If the planner charges an hourly fee, ask them to agree to a maximum fee for the services you need or ask them to notify you before their bill exceeds a certain limit. Most professionals who provide services on an hourly basis are very comfortable with their rates, and they should be able to provide a good estimate of the time needed for the job. Generally speaking, their rates have to be fair. If they are too high, they risk losing new business. Too low, and they may not provide the comprehensive services you desire. If they are only providing investment management, the total hourly fee should not exceed an amount equal to one percent of the value of your portfolio. As an example, if you have $250,000 then the total hourly fees charged should not exceed $2,500 in any given year. If you have a more substantial amount, you should expect a lower fee in percentage terms. Include the value of all of the assets they review in this calculation, like 401k's, which they may not actually manage directly but still provide advice.

Some planners and advisors use a flat fee. Firms charging flat fees, sometimes called retainer fees, charge all clients a flat amount. For instance, a firm might charge all clients an annual fee of $10,000 and provide most services under this flat fee. If they offer ancillary services that are one-time in nature, like assistance with an unusual asset sale or the sale of a business, they may charge an additional flat or hourly fee. The advantage of a flat fee for you is that you know what you are paying regardless of the growth or lack of growth in your account values. The advisor who uses flat fees knows their income will not fluctuate as long as they do a good job for their clients! Although some firms are beginning to use flat fees, it is still not common. Most firms, particularly those offering investment management, charge a percentage of assets under management.

Fees that are based on a percentage of assets under management may be either a flat percentage or a tiered fee schedule, which results in a lower percentage fee as your assets grow. As an example, a firm may charge all clients 1 percent or it may charge 1.5 percent of the first $500,000, 1.25 percent of the next $500,000, 1 percent of the next million, and .4 percent for the portion above $2,000,000. If you had a $3,000,000 account under this tiered schedule, your fee would be .925 percent, or $27,750 per year. Clients who pay a tiered schedule should recognize as their account grows in value, the percentage they are charged gets lower. If their account falls in value, their fee in dollars drops, but the percentage that they are paying actually is higher. Basically, it is exactly the opposite of the United States federal income tax!

It is important to discuss compensation with any financial professional involved in assisting you with your financial needs. You should know why they chose their specific method and how the total costs compare to those of other advisors. Regardless of the compensation method, you should be convinced the value you receive is worth the costs. You should make sure the fee is fair and not above the average amount charged by other advisors. Finally, if there are multiple professionals from different firms involved with you, you need to make sure that all compensation-sharing arrangements are fully disclosed. If you are considering a financial professional and they do not willingly share their source and method of compensation, do not hire them.

Services

You need to know what services your financial professional is willing to offer you. Some professionals choose to become specialists and offer only one service. Some work within firms providing all of the financial services any client could possibly need. Some of the services firms offer include:

- Cash Management and Budgeting
- Education Planning
- Income Tax Planning and Preparation
- Estate Tax Planning and Preparation
- Estate, Retirement, and Income Planning
- Investment Review and Planning
- Investment Management
- Insurance Planning and Product Sales

For each service, ask your prospective advisor if you will work with them regardless of the service provided or if they plan to assign a specialist for certain services. For those that "do it all," make sure they have the experience and training necessary to provide all of the services to you. The financial world has become more complicated and most professionals do not want to provide all services directly. Do not hesitate to work with someone who offers only a few of the services listed above, assuming they provide the services you need.

As a matter of fact, you should work with a primary contact who brings in other members of their firm, or from outside their firm, for those services they do not offer. There is real value in having a team that is composed of your attorney, accountant, and financial professional. This is especially important regardless of your net worth. As mentioned earlier, a team approach is only valid when your team of professionals is truly independent. It is perfectly acceptable for your attorney and investment advisor to refer business to each other and share many clients. But make sure at least one of your team members is independent.

Obviously, if a professional does not offer the services you need, you should ask them to recommend someone who does. Many financial professionals belong to professional organizations that have members with many different specialties. If anyone refers you to someone, ask them to disclose any compensation arrangements to you in writing.

Compliance

Whether you work with an investment advisor, broker, insurance agent, accountant or attorney, all are regulated. It is critical that the person you hire, and their firm, have integrity. For investment advisors, the Form ADV Part II and Schedule F contain any violations by the firm and all investment advisor representatives of the firm. They should provide one to you, but you can also find the firm through the SEC website at www.sec.gov. You should check the SEC website prior to hiring any investment advisor!

For brokers, you need to review their U-4. A sample U-4 is in the appendix for reference. You can also independently access their compliance record at www.finra.com/brokercheck. The State Corporation Commission Department of Insurance will have records for any insurance agent, or agency, operating within your state. A listing of your State's Department of Insurance addresses, phone numbers, and websites is available at www.naic.org.

If they hold designations, you can also check with the issuer of the designation to make sure they have the designation and a clean record.

You should have total confidence in both the individual and the firm you decide to hire. They should have integrity and a clean record. If not, you need to look elsewhere.

Independence

Independence is what you want your advisor to have as they work with you. But, in this case, it is your independence that is important when you hire an advisor. You must have independence after you hire a professional to help you.

Here is a more direct statement about the need for your independence: Do not hire anyone you cannot also fire without ancillary repercussions! This means you should not hire immediate family, someone from your club or church, the next-door neighbor, or, heaven forbid, any in-law! The last thing anyone needs is to be in a divorce with their soon to be ex-father-in-law managing their money! Once you hire anybody fitting this description, you are going to have a tough time firing them.

Do not hire anyone you cannot also fire without ancillary repercussions.

Find a person who can work with you on a professional basis. If they join your church or club in a few years, you don't need to fire them. But please do not hire anyone who already has this type of relationship with you. It can become very awkward if things do not work out.

Chemistry

Assuming your prospective advisor passed the previous criteria, the final and most important consideration is chemistry. It takes a significant amount of time to determine your prospective advisor has the necessary experience, compensation method, services available, and clean record of regulatory compliance, and you know you can fire them if things don't work out. Once they have satisfied all of these criteria, you should know them fairly well. It should not take long for you to determine if they pass the most important characteristic you should look for in an advisor – chemistry!

You do not have to find the "perfect" advisor, but you shouldn't work with someone with whom you really don't enjoy spending time. You may not see your advisor every day, but you shouldn't dread seeing them, either! It may surprise you, but many advisors prefer to work with clients who they like and look forward to seeing.

By the time you decide an advisor has passed all of the other criteria, if the chemistry is not a match, then the chances are the advisor senses that the two of you do not "click". If they are very experienced, they probably are already anticipating, or in extreme cases, they are hoping that you will look elsewhere. With no offense intended, they may be hoping you will move on and it is even possible they will tell you to look elsewhere.

If they are like most advisors, they also may know of someone who would work well with you. It may sound odd, but an honest discussion with them might result in their referral to an advisor more appropriate for you. Remember most competent advisors know and often network with their "competition." Remember the "wrong advisor" is very competent; they just are not appropriate for you. You should anticipate a professional response to your decision not to hire them, and, if your discussion results in pressure then you just received confirmation you really should not work with them. Move on.

The appendix includes an advisor questionnaire like the one shown below. It is also available for free as a download from www.investiphobia.com Use it, and remember, you are hoping to hire an experienced professional to handle your assets. Add questions you feel are important and let me know of any you believe apply to other investors! Even though an advisor may know more than you do about your finances and your investments, they are not you and they do not own your investments! Always remember, you are the boss!

Conclusion

Behavioral economics combines psychology and the study of human behavior with finance and the study of economics.

For decades, we have assumed that investors (including ourselves) were rational. Investors are human. Human beings are rational, some of the time. Why would anyone assume we are rational all of the time?

That's one irrational assumption.

Modern Portfolio Theory and The Efficient Market Hypothesis are still valid approaches to understanding the financial markets. They should not be discarded simply because it turns out that the players in those markets are just as human as you are.

Most of them, anyway.

However — our fears, especially those which paralyze us, have a profound effect on the decisions we make (or refuse to make) in regard to our investments.

There are eighteen fears that will cause *investiphobia* if we fail to effectively address them:

1. The Fear of Losing Your Investment
2. The Fear of Losing Your Income
3. The Fear of Losing Spending Power

4. The Fear of Thinking Long Term
5. The Fear of Losing Control
6. The Fear of Not Keeping Up with the Joneses
7. The Fear of Making Mistakes
8. The Fear of Buying the Wrong Product
9. The Fear of Buying/Selling at the Wrong Time
10. The Fear of Getting Taken
11. The Fear of Bad Advice
12. The Fear of Change
13. The Fear of Diagnosis
14. The Fear of Taxes and the IRS
15. The Fear of Losing Access to Your Money
16. The Fear of Disappointing Parents
17. The Fear of Disappointing Children
18. The Fear of Choosing the Wrong Advisor

Investiphobia is ongoing, continuous, and contagious. It will rear its ugly head no matter what the market is doing. No kidding — I've encountered (in my prospects and clients) every fear described in this book during upwardly-moving markets! Investiphobic investors allow their fears to manage their portfolios, regardless of market conditions. They are no more investiphobic now than they were in the late 1990's or from 2003-2006 when the market was surging. If the current market causes you to have any of the fears that lead to investiphobia, do not wait for the market to change, thinking they'll go away on their own.

The treatment of any form of *investiphobia* must be based on the fear that caused it in the first place. In most cases, the best cure is finding and retaining the right advisor — one with whom you have great chemistry, who represents only your best interests, and can fully explain any course of action in a way that you completely understand. That person is going to be a on the same side of the table with you and will design a portfolio that fully and effectively addresses each of your fears. You will know you've made the right choice if your *investiphobia* begins to fade over a reasonable period of time.

So, I encourage you to use the questionnaire at the end of this book and spend the time necessary to make sure you choose an advisor you can trust.

If you know of a fear that you think should have been included in this book, please let me know. You can reach me by email at paul@investiphobia.net. This book also has a website, www.investiphobia.com. Check it periodically for updates and commentary on the treatment of fears addressed in this book.

There is no information on the many different ways an advisor can manage your money within this book because a detailed discussion of a particular investment philosophy would detract from the primary message of the book. Investors are human and our beliefs are not the same. Rather than specifying a particular investment method, it is more important to recognize the importance of having, and understanding, a philosophy or strategy you believe in. Investiphobia is not an issue of investment strategy, but it can be caused by investors participating in an investment approach that differs from their own belief system. Socially Responsible Investing(SRI) is one method investors may use to bring their portfolio into sync with their personal beliefs. More "values-based" approaches are needed to reflect the wide variety of individual human values.

Now, I hope you will act on what you've just finished reading. Having lived with fear for many years, I speak from my own personal experience when I say, you can live without fear. And, you can invest too!

After all — what's there to fear?

Author's Note

Losing money can really make someone angry, but, intellectually, they know they can make up the losses over time. But, when time is lost you know you will never get it back. When it comes to time versus money, time is the more important asset!

This made me think of how the financial industry calculates investment performance. The factor of time, in many of these calculations is limited to the time period of the investment, e.g. One Year, Year To Date, Trailing Three Years, Calendar Year, etc. What about the time you spend as an investor? Isn't that part of your whole return?

When we invest our time, we should be rewarded. If you knew you could receive a comparable monetary return on your investments without spending any of your personal time, wouldn't that mean your return is higher? You have the same amount in dollars, but more time to do the things you would like to do.

Total return includes income and the gain or loss of an investment over a period of time. I propose a new calculation, one that considers the Whole Investor. The Whole Return is the income, plus the gain or loss, over a given time period divided by the amount of time you spent, as an investor, generating the return. This calculation may also need to consider the satisfaction factor that comes from matching your investments with your philosophy and beliefs. Shouldn't your return include more than money? It may not be easy, but you can make up your losses when it comes to money. But time, well, you do not know how much time you have and the time you lose can never be replaced!

Perhaps including your time, satisfaction, and your fears in your return calculation would more accurately reflect your "whole" return.

Appendix
Advisor Questionnaire

How to Choose the "Right" Advisor For You

Credentials/Designations

What are your Certifications and Designations?

Chartered Financial Analyst(CFA) ___

Certified Financial Planner(CPF) ___

Chartered Financial Consultant(ChFC) ___

Certified Investment Management Analyst(CIMA) ___

Chartered Life Underwriter(CLU) ___

Certified Public Accountant(CPA) ___

Personal Financial Specialist(PFS)

___

Other ______________________________

Tell me how you chose to pursue your designation(s) and what they mean to you.

____

____

____

Memberships

Financial Planning Association (FPA) ___

National Association of Personal Financial Advisors(NAPFA)

___

Investment Management Consultants Association(IMCA) ___

Other____

____

____

Education

College Degree Y / N Major:____________________________

Graduate Degree Y / N Major:____________________________

Colleges attended___

____

Other___________________________

Experience

How long have you been in the financial services industry?

In which of the following areas do you have experience:

Area of Experience	**Years of Experience**
Cash Management and Budgeting	
Investment Review and Planning	
Income Tax Planning and Preparation	
Estate Planning	
Life Insurance Planning	
Long-Term Care Insurance Planning	
Retirement Income Planning	
Charitable Gift Planning	
Other:__________________________	

Compensation

Is your compensation Fee Only?

Do you receive commissions, solicitation fees, or finder's fees for any products that you recommend?

How are fees calculated, hourly, flat/retainer, as a percentage, or a combination?

Please describe:

Is your compensation Commission Only?

Do you disclose the commission rate and anticipated commission for the products you sell? If not, why not?

Is your compensation Fee Based?(Combination of Fee and Commission)?

How do you decide whether to offer commission or fee based solutions?

For which services do you charge fees?

How are the fees calculated, hourly, flat/retainer, as a percentage, or a combination?

Please describe:

For which services is your compensation in the form of commissions?

Do you disclose the commission rate and anticipated commission for the products you sell? If not, why not?

Regardless of your compensation type, does anyone else receive compensation from you or your firm as a result of any services or products that you provide?
If yes, who else receives compensation, how much, and why?

Services Offered

Area of Experience	Fee or Commission	
Cash Management and Budgeting		
Investment Review and Planning		
Income Tax Planning and Preparation		
Estate Planning		
Life Insurance Planning		
Long-Term Care Insurance Planning		
Retirement Income Planning		
Charitable Gift Planning		
Other:		

Do you accept fiduciary responsibility for your services?
Will you provide me with a comprehensive written analysis, plan, and recommended actions?
Will you assist me in implementing your recommendations?
Do you have access to all of the products that may be needed?
How do you select the products that you recommend?
If you are selected to manage any investments, do you offer discretionary management? ___non-discretionary management?___

Do you or your firm have any custody of the investments? Where do you typically recommend your clients to hold their investments? Why?

Regulatory Compliance

1 Are you a registered representative of a brokerage firm?
If yes, are you an Investment Advisor representative of your firms registered investment advisor?
If yes, how do you decide whether to recommend fee-based investment advisory services or traditional commission-based product sales?
If yes, are you also licensed as an insurance agent?
If yes, do you sell variable life and annuity products?

2 Are you an Investment Advisor Representative of a state or SEC Registered Investment Advisor?
If yes, are you also licensed as an insurance agent?
If yes, do you have access to no load variable life and annuity products?
If yes, may I have a copy of your firm's Form ADV Part II and Schedule F?

Questions below are for you to answer, not the prospective advisor?

Independence

Does the individual or the firm have any connection to your personal life?

Did any of your friends recommend the firm?
Is the individual a member of any group in which you are also a member?

If the answer to any of the above questions is yes, then, if you hire this advisor and become dissatisfied, will you need to apologize to anyone for firing them?

Chemistry

Do you like this advisor?

Do you enjoy spending time with them?

Do you believe that you will feel more comfortable about your financial situation if you hire them?

Appendix
Recommended Websites

Whole Investor Network
www.wholeinvestor.com - The website for the publisher of the Investiphobia Book Series providing additional links and educational materials for investors and financial services professionals. Author contact information, speaking information, and additional program materials are available on this website. This website also contains all links referenced in this appendix.

CFP Board of Standards
www.cfp.net
The mission of Certified Financial Planner Board of Standards, Inc. is to benefit the public by granting the CFP® certification and upholding it as the recognized standard of excellence for personal financial planning.

CFA Institute
www.cfainstitute.org
CFA Institute is a global, not-for-profit organization comprising the world's largest association of investment professionals. With over 100,000 members, and regional societies around the world, we are dedicated to developing and promoting the

highest educational, ethical, and professional standards in the investment industry.

FI360

www.fi360.com - Fiduciary 360 website provides information to investors, retirement plan participants, and industry participants regarding fiduciary issues for trusts, retirement plans, and charitable funds. A list of AIF and AIFA certificants is on this website.

Financial Industry Regulatory Authority

www.finra.org - The Self-Regulatory Agency overseeing the Brokerage Industry

www.finra.org/brokercheck - Provides specific information about registered representatives and broker dealers

Kinder Institute

www.kinderinstitute.com - Provides information about life planning and a directory of Registered Life Planners.

My Money

www.MyMoney.gov - The U.S. Governments website to help citizens learn about money.

National Association of Estate Planning Attorneys

www.naepc.org - Provides information and a directory of Estate Planning Attorneys

National Association of Insurance Commissioners
www.naic.org
http://www.naic.org/state_web_map.htm - Provides updated list of State Departments of Insurance from the National Association of Insurance Commissioners. Their main website has links to excellent consumer guides on insurance products.

Securities and Exchange Commission
www.sec.gov
www.adviserinfo.sec.gov/IAPD/Content/IapdMain/iapd_SiteMap.aspx
www.usa.gov/Citizen/Topics/Money/Personal_Finance.shtml

Books Referenced in Investiphobia

Ariely, Dan. Predictably Irrational, Revised and Expanded Edition: The Hidden Forces That Shape Our Decisions, Harper Perennial, 2010.

Bogle, John C., *Enough: true measures of money, business, and life.* Wiley, 2010.

Brafman, Ori; Brafman, Ram. Sway: The Irresistible Pull of Irrational Behavior. Broadway Business, 2009.

Darst, David. The Little Book that Saves Your Assets. Wiley, 2008.

Evensky, Harold; Katz, Deena B., Retirement Income Redesigned: Master Plans for Distribution. Bloomberg Press, 2006.

Ferguson, Niall. The Ascent of Money. Penguin, 2009.

Fox, Justin. The Myth of the Rational Market. HarperBusiness, 2009.

Gwaltney, James; Stroup, Richard L.; Lee, Dwight; Common Sense Economics: What Everyone Should Know About Wealth and Prosperity. St. Martin's Press, 2005.

Kinder, George. The Seven Stages of Money Maturity: Understanding the Spirit and Value of Money in Your Life. Dell, 2000.

Krueger, David. Mann, John David. The Secret Language of Money: How to Make Smarter Financial Decisions and Live a Richer Life, McGraw Hill, 2009.

Levitt, Steven D. Dubner; Stephen J., Freakonomics: A Rogue Economist Explores the Hidden Side of Everything. Harper Perennial, 2009.

Levitt, Steven D. Dubner; Stephen J. SuperFreakonomics: Global Cooling, Patriotic Prostitutes, and Why Suicide Bombers should buy Life Insurance. William Morrow, 2009.

Markopolous, Harry. No One Would Listen. Wiley, 2010.

Shefrin, Herb. Beyond Greed and Fear: Understanding Behavioral Finance and the Psychology of Investing. Oxford University Press, 2007.

Shiller, Robert. Irrational Exuberance, Crown, 2006.

Thaler, Richard. Susstein, Cass. Nudge: Improving Decisions About Health, Wealth, and Happiness, Penguin, 2009.

Acknowledgements

Writing a book is a very interesting process. It takes time to develop an idea, put it into words, and hone those words into a cogent and understandable message. Throughout the process, editors work with authors to eliminate unnecessary words and to bring a consistency of style to the manuscript. I had the pleasure of working with an experienced executive editor, Ralph Rieves, and his team at Farragut, Jones, and Lawrence. Ralph and Doug Schmidt worked diligently to bring *Investiphobia: Overcome Your Deepest Investment Fear!* to fruition.

Thank you to:

My daughters Hillary and Darby for their encouragement and positive attitude about their Dad writing a book and for reminding me that everyone can be anything they want to be, as long as they are willing to do what it takes.

Kathy Lowery and Jack Lynch for suggesting, in Italy, that I should write a book!

Judith for all of her sound advice and for listening.

My friend and former manager at Jefferson Pilot Securities Corporation, Hughes B. "Pete" Perry, for an enjoyable afternoon of pool and for coining the title word, Investiphobia.

My clients for their encouragement and their faith in me.

To the staff and crew of all of the Starbucks I visited while writing this book, particularly Luis, Megan, and Amber and their crew at the Shore Drive location in Virginia Beach, and to the friendly people in line and on the deck for listening and giving me tips.

To the Sports Bar and also La Perla in Recco, Italy, for the best espresso, possibly on the planet, and for putting up with my butchering of the Italian language.

To my mom, who passed away in 1994, thank you for writing your own book, Prunes, Pride, and Vinegar Pie and Music, Music, Music. Mom always said I should write a book.

To my dad, for his encouragement and support.

To Kim for getting me on the plane to Italy, helping me address my own fears, inspiring me to write the book, for the initial editing, and for making me feel so very happy! Finally, to you the reader, I hope you enjoyed reading the book and that it gives you the ability to invest without fear.

Thank you!

If you liked,

Investiphobia: Overcome Your Deepest Investment Fears

You may also enjoy:

Eat, sleep, spend money. It's the American Way.· This light and entertaining book explores how our emotions keep us from making good money choices.

The revolutionary consumer-oriented book shows how we think and feel about money and how our emotions impact our spending decisions.· Money success is about behavior; not about product selection ("Financial Stuff" to use the author's words).

Compelling vignettes surround a story of taking "A Trip To The Mall" and offer a light and entertaining account of how our human nature conspires against us when we make money choices

For More Information

www.myapexx.com

7848960R0

Made in the USA
Charleston, SC
15 April 2011